POMPEII · NAPLES

VESUVIUS-HERCULANEUM-VILLA OF THE PAPYRI-OPLONTIS
SORRENTO-POSITANO-AMALFI-RAVELLO-CETARA
VIETRI SUL MARE-PAESTUM-CAPRI-ISCHIA

D0768149

270 COLOR PHOTOS · PLAN OF NAPLES
PLAN OF THE EXCAVATIONS OF POMPEII AND OF HERCULANEUM

BONECHI EDIZIONI "IL TURISMO"

Authorized distributing agent for Naples and Campania:
VERBEL S.a.s. di Mariarosaria Bello & C.
Via Domenico Quaranta, 23
80126 Loggetta (NA)
Tel. +39-081.593.94.46
E-mail: verbelsas@libero.it

© Copyright 2005 by Bonechi - Edizioni "Il Turismo" S.r.l.
Via G. Di Vittorio, 31 - 50145 Florence
Tel. +39-055.375739/3424527
Fax +39-055.374701
E-mail: bbonechi@dada.it
        info@bonechionline.com
http://www.bonechionline.com
All rights reserved
Printed in Italy

Publishing editor: Barbara Bonechi
Graphic design and layout: Sabrina Menicacci
Maps, photo retouching and cover: Paola Rufino
Drawing Villa of the Papyri, pages 110-111: kindly granted by Virgilio Galati
Texts of Pompeii, Herculaneum, Villa of the Papyri, Oplontis: edited by Ferruccio Canali
Texts of Positano, Ravello, Cetara, Vietri sul Mare: edited by Dr. Giuliano Valdes
Photographs: Archives of Bonechi - Edizioni "Il Turismo" S.r.l.; Casa Editrice V. Carcavallo (Naples);
Mario Pirone (Naples); Mimmo Jodice (Naples); Nicola Grifoni (Florence); Mauro Caiano (Naples);
Fotostudio Piero Orlandi (Lainate - Milan);
kindly granted by: Ferruccio Canali e Virgilio Galati (Florence)
Photolithography: Studio Leonardo Fotolito S.r.l., Florence
Printing: Petruzzi Stampa, Città di Castello (PG)

ISBN: 88-7204-557-6

*The location of the artworks in this book corresponds to their whereabouts as the book goes to press.
* Everything possible has been done to ascertain the legitimate owners of the rights for individual illustrations. In case there have been any involuntary omissions, we will be happy to pay the user fees.

POMPEII

I t's hard to tell exactly what the origins of ancient Pompeii were and even whether the name is of Greek or of Italic derivation. The generally accepted version is that it might come from the Greek "pémpo, pompé" or the Oscan "pompe" (the city was probably founded by the Oscans who were the dominant peoples in Campania). The first sure notice we have dates to the 6th century BC when it was already a real town surrounded by solid walls. The geographical position, on a height overlooking the plain where the river meets the sea and forms a convenient landing point for Phoenician and Greek navigators and traders, leads us to believe that there must have been something there as early as the 8th century BC, perhaps simply a small settlement of people who farmed the Sarno valley. The Greeks, who had set up bases in Cumae and taken over the entire gulf of Naples up to Sorrento, Capri and Ischia, hoped to bring Pompeii into the orbit of the powerful state of Cumae, despite opposition from the Etruscan lords of the Campanian hinterland. In order to survive Pompeii was forced to ally itself commercially and politically with the Greeks of Cumae, although the Etruscans

▼ *Via di Mercurio and the Tower of Mercury, as they were two thousand years ago, seen from the Arch of Caligula*

momentarily regained the upper hand, taking back the positions they had lost between 525 and 474 BC, at least until their fleet was defeated by the Greeks and the city once more came under Hellenic hegemony. The Pompeians were not organized to defend themselves from Etruscans and Greeks and could not hope to remain independent. In the 5th century BC when the Samnites, an Oscan tribe of the interior, from Irpinia and Sannio, defeated the Greeks and the Etruscans, Pompeii had to submit to the new lords. From then on the city was governed according to Samnite customs and laws, and absorbed their language and religion.

Not much is known concerning the life of the city in the period of Samnite supremacy. However in the year 310 BC Pompeians and Nucerians were compelled to take up arms to defend themselves from the incursions of the Roman fleet, which put ashore its men at the mouth of the Sarno and pillaged the coast. Rome, now powerful, defeated the Samnites and Pompeii was forced into a sort of league with the Roman state that however left her a certain independence. Pompeii tried to regain her liberty during the Social War siding with the Italic allies, but when they were defeated at Nola Pompeii officially became a military colony "Cornelia Veneria Pom-

peianorum" (80 BC). It was no easy thing for the Romans to suppress these differences of a political, economic and social nature, but as time went on the Pompeians were romanized, accepting the language, customs, legislation and municipal regulations of Rome.

In his Annals Tacitus tells us something about the character of the Pompeians of the time when he describes the tragic riot that exploded between Pompeians and Nucerians during a gladiatorial contest in the Amphitheater. The year was AD 59 and two pairs of gladiators – one local and the other from Nocera – were competing in the arena. The crowd was wild and, as

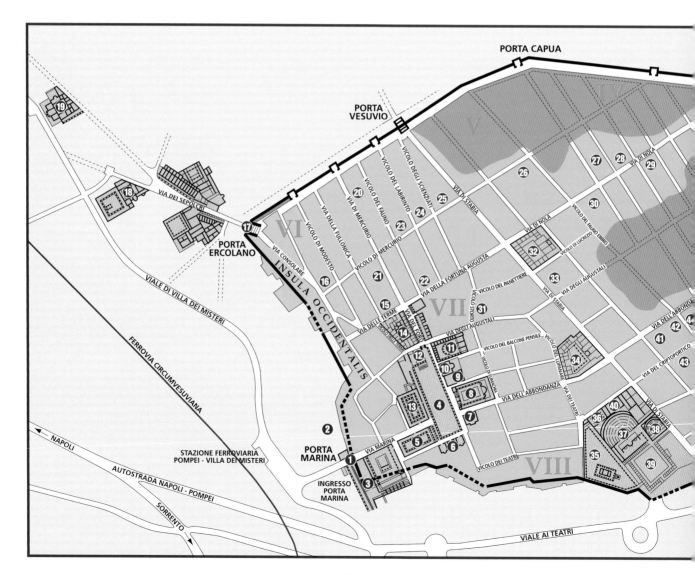

usual in sport contests, incited both pairs. Evidently some fan of the local pair had made a disparaging remark about the adversary and this led to a row that then degenerated into a general riot, concluding with the massacre of whatever Nucerian was unlucky enough to fall into the hands of the Pompeians. The news got to Rome and Nero expounded it to the Senate where measures were taken to close the amphitheater for ten years.

Like the neighboring cities, Pompeii rose on the slopes of Mt. Vesuvius in an area particularly subject to earthquakes and the dangers of volcanic eruptions. The first premonitory sign of the tragedy that

was to strike Pompeii was the fearful earthquake of AD 62. The city, like many others in Campania, was seriously damaged. Once the fear of another earthquake had passed, works of reconstruction and renewal of the temples, public and private buildings went swiftly forward. The city was enriched with new patrician homes, workshops and shops thanks to its economic, commercial and industrial power. But seventeen years later, on August 24th, in AD 79, shortly after noon, the appalling catastrophe took place. Mt. Vesuvius erupted and literally buried the city (together with Herculaneum and Stabiae) under a layer between six and seven meters

deep of ashes, small volcanic stones and other eruptive material. Very few managed to escape. Most of the population, at the time probably around twenty thousand, died suffocated in the streets, homes and cellars where many thought they would be safe from the destructive fury of the fire and the poisonous fumes. We are left aghast when we observe the plaster casts made from the empty spaces left in the hard shells of ashes and small volcanic stones by the bodies of those who died so horribly. Pliny the Elder came with the fleet, based in Miseno, to succor the Pompeians. He was not only an admiral but also a famous scholar of natural

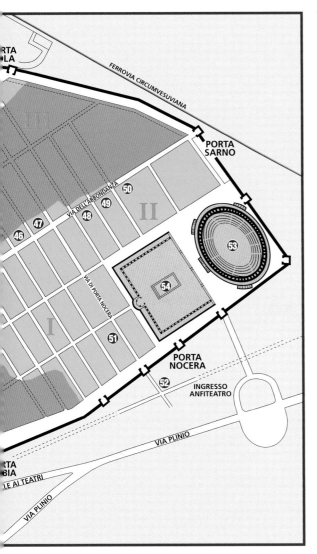

▲ Bird's-eye view of the area of the Forum

phenomena. But he could do nothing and his scientific interest in studying the eruption first hand resulted in his death. What we do know comes from two dramatic letters sent by his nephew Pliny the Younger to Tacitus. As time passed and the eruptions continued, Pompeii passed into oblivion, and for centuries, despite the letters of Pliny the Younger, no one knew exactly where the city was located. Even when, between 1594 and 1600, the architect Domenico Fontana discovered ruins and inscriptions in digging for the construction of a canal to bring water from the Sarno River to Torre Annunziata, it was not established that it was Pompeii. In 1748 King Charles of Bourbon made the first trial digs, which consisted mostly of simple tunnels so that the objects and statues so avidly collected could be removed from the homes. Between 1815 and 1832 the Forum, the Basilica, the House of the Faun, that of the Tragic Poet, of Pansa and the Forum Baths were uncovered. Then between 1850 and 1859 the Stabian Baths came to the light. Once the Kingdom of Italy was declared, in 1860 the direction of the excavations was entrusted to Giuseppe Fiorelli, whose methods were strictly scientific. His was the idea of making casts by pouring liquid plaster into the hollows left in the ashes by the victims and the various wooden objects. After Fiorelli other distinguished archaeologists perfected excavation methods. These included Michele Ruggiero, Giulio De Petra, Antonio Sogliano and Vittorio Spinazzola. It was Amedeo Maiuri who brought the excavations to what they are today, uncovering three-fifths of the area of the city between 1924 and 1962. Those who wish to delve in depth into the secrets of the archaeological digs in Campania can do so by turning to his many writings.

The urban structure of the City

As the thick layer of ashes and volcanic stones was gradually removed, archaeologists were astonished by the distinctive town plan that came to light, unlike those in other Roman cities. Pompeii was under the sway of various peoples: Etruscan, Greek, Samnite, Roman in addition to the original Italic peoples who must have founded the first urban center, on the site of the present Forum. The city is thus characterized by varied types of urban structures in which the techniques and building materials reflect the customs and styles of each rule. The various phases identified begin with the 8th-7th century BC, when Pompeii was settled by local agrarian populations of the Sarno valley (no building as such has been identified, except perhaps traces in the Temple of Apollo in the Forum), followed by the 6th century BC, first period of Greek hegemony (parts of the oldest city walls); 525-474 BC, Etruscan dominion (parts of the temple in the Triangular Forum); 474-425 BC, second Greek hegemony, with the renovation of the archaic Doric temple and above all the so-called Triangular Forum; 4th-3rd century BC, first Samnite phase; 200-80 BC, second Samnite phase, in which Hellenistic influences came to the fore; 80 BC-AD 14, first Ro-

man period, Republican and Augustan; AD 14-AD 79, second Roman period, early Empire, coinciding with the Claudian and Flavian ages. Since vast parts of Pompeii are still buried, each excavation campaign brings to light something new and, above all, permits us to reconsider previous information, at times overthrowing current convictions. This is what happened in the 2001-2003 excavation campaign carried out in Regio VI, where a 3rd century BC settlement was unearthed (Samnite period), furnishing us with a picture of the city in a period that had up to

then been little known. The new finds have demonstrated that the town plan of Pompeii, which remained practically unchanged up to the end of the city in AD 79, goes back to around 300 BC, reflecting the Italic-Republican layout. The urban configuration, the walls, most of the buildings, and the paintings date to a period between the 3rd and the 1st century BC, eliminating the previously held conviction, popular among scholars, that the city was an important example of the architectural and artistic culture of the period of Imperial Rome (on the contrary, Pompeii

▶ *A stretch of Via dell'Abbondanza; the large stones in the foreground served as crossing stones for pedestrians*

in AD 79, that is in the early Empire, was a provincial center, still bound to a rationale typical of settlements and architectural dynamics dating to earlier centuries and that, with few exceptions, lagged behind new developments in the capital. Each of the settlement phases from the 6th to the 1st century BC had its own way of building, using different materials and techniques that depended on acquired experience. Scholars have therefore been able to identify the various phases of the city's urban and building transformation. Samnite and Republican Rome have of course left the greatest mark, but unlike the prototype of the "square city" in line with the dictates of Roman military town planning, here the conformation of the land with the city on a bastion of prehistoric lava origins almost 40 meters above sea level, obliged the "town planners" to follow the lay of the land. There is a considerable slope from north to south, while the flat part is located at the western extremity of the city. It is in this flat part that the most important public buildings are situated, while the real town center consists of the cluster of houses arranged in blocks, with straight streets. With their narrow sidewalks, these streets cross each other at right angles and are characterized by fountains at the crossings and large stepping-stones every so often to make crossing easier for the pedestrian. The Triangular Forum and the theaters were lo-

▼ *The Macellum, the old covered market, with the Forum portico in front*

◀ *The Suburban Baths in the quarter of the same name*

member. This interesting aspect of what has often been called the "dead city" shows us how far from the truth such a definition is. The life that the appalling catastrophe brought to an abrupt halt is set before us with an immediacy that makes the city live again. In this reawakening the history and civilization of Pompeii continue to reverberate throughout the world thanks to the multitudes of visitors who come there every year.

To help the visitor orient himself and identify the various itineraries and buildings, archaeologists have divided the built-up area into 9 regions, each subdivided into blocks (*insulae*), with a progressive number to every entrance in every block.

cated in the far southern residential sector, while the large amphitheater and the palaestra were in the far southeastern sector. The fortification walls are three kilometers and 220 meters long; the built-up area measures 66 hectares. What really make the city come alive for us are the many inscriptions still extant, a real *vademecum* (guide) to city life. As the excavation progressed these inscriptions scratched or painted on the plaster walls were collected and deciphered, since they were subject to loss by atmospheric agents or for other reasons. Painted in large black or red letters, or incised in normal letters with a stylus, most of these wall inscriptions were of an advertising nature, referring to performances in the amphitheater, notices of houses for rent, lost objects, encouraging

the citizens in election times to vote for a specific candidate, workshop and tavern shop signs. In places frequented by a varied crowd, such as shops, the amphitheater, houses, the inscriptions referred to debts, cash receipts, promises of love, or consisted of obscene phrases, caricatures, business dates to re-

▶ *The fountain of Abundance, after which the main street of Pompeii was named*

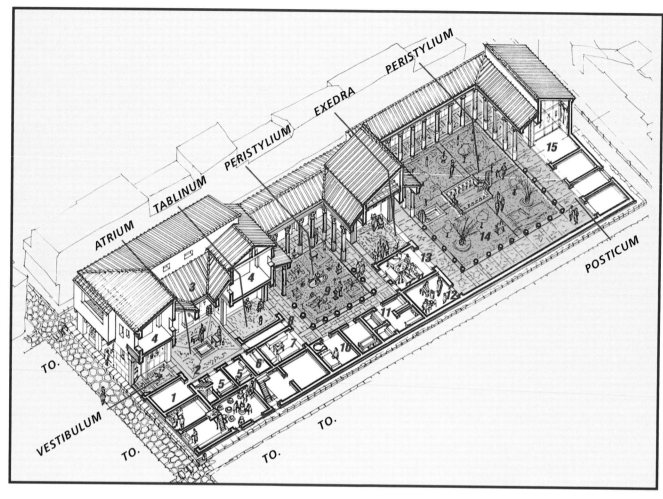

TO. Tabernae and Officinae
1 Atriensis
2 Impluvium
3 Compluvium
4 Upper floor
5 Cubicula

6 Ala
7 Triclinium
8 Andron
9 Viridarium and Peristylium
10 Kitchen
11 Balneum

12 Gynaeceum
13 Triclinii, Exedrae and other rooms
   used during the day
14 Second Peristylium with garden
15 Oecus and Dietae,
   rooms for daily use

The Pompeian House and its decoration

The buildings, like the city plan, reflect the successive dominions, and the individual complexes were frequently transformed and stratified in the course of the various phases.

Since the Italic-Roman building element predominates (although with a strong Greek influence), it behooves us to take a look at the plan of the famous *House of the Vettii*, which furnishes us a clear and precise idea of the interior layout and the various rooms in which most of the patrician houses were divided. At the same time it gives us a chance to become acquainted with the terminology of the various parts (to be found also in other dwellings). The first thing to note is that the house was enclosed in high windowless walls, almost as if it were a fortress hiding whatever went on inside from sight and providing the inhabitants with absolute privacy.

Names of the various rooms. *Vestibule*: the space right at the entrance door to the house, projecting from the wall, which owes its name to the fact that it is sacred to the goddess Vesta. *Fauces*: the passageway leading to the atrium. *Atrium*: a rectangular open room, typical of the Italic house (perhaps of Etruscan origin), around which the living

▶ *The exedra and the peristyles of the House of the Faun*

quarters open. The *atrium* was in a sense the busiest room in the house where domestic life took place (in other houses, at the back, is the *tablinum*, where the lord of the house lived and slept. This was later turned into a reception hall). The atrium gradually evolved into a courtyard covered by a roof on pillars and columns, and thus became a portico, known as *tetrastyle* if the columns were four (one at each corner), and Corinthian if there were more columns (*Vitruvius*). Rain entered through the open space at the center of the roof, the *compluvium*, and was collected in the *impluvium* or basin in the middle of the *atrium*. After the atrium comes the *peri-style*, a large courtyard surrounded by porticoes, within which was the garden with fountains and statues. Then there were the *cubicula*, or bedrooms, and the *triclinium*, the dining room with three couches (*clinai*) on which the diners (generally three to a couch) reclined along three sides of the table, leaving the fourth side free for serving. It is to be noted that in the patrician dwellings there is more than one

▼ *Paintings in the oecus of the House of the Vettii*

◄ *Mosaic with marine fauna, in the Archaeological Museum in Naples*

ings, paintings, mosaics and small sculptures in bronze and marble, all of which tell us much about the development of the artists as well as of the craftsmen, who delighted in making all kinds of useful objects, bronze vases, and fine pieces of silver. The wall paintings of Pompeii and Herculaneum are of prime importance, for any discussion of Roman painting refers almost exclusively to them. The frescoes from the Villa of Mysteries and many other fine examples in the Archaeological Museum of Naples reveal the characteristics of the individual artists, even though they remain nameless. Wall painting is divided into four styles: the *First Style* is known as "incrusted" because the surface of the stucco walls is divided into colored rectangles, imitations of colored marbleized panels. Sometimes also called "structural" style, it echoed Hellenistic fashions and lasted till around the middle of the 1st century BC. The *Second Style* is characterized by "perspective architecture", in which the various architectural elements such as socles, columns, cornices, architraves, porticoes were painted on the walls and appeared to project out towards the observer. Landscapes or figured compositions were painted in the areas they framed. This style, also known as "architectural", was fashionable from the first half to the end of the 1st century BC. The *Third Style* known as "of the real wall" or "ornamental" is derived from the pre-

"*triclinium*" or day room, located in different parts of the house so that as the seasons changed there would always be a room that was cool in summer and warmed by the sun in winter. The *alae* are generally two rooms on either side of the atrium. In the houses of the wealthy they may possibly have held the ancestor images. Then the *oecus*, the most intimate rooms from the point of view of decoration. The various architectural orders – Doric, Ionic, Corinthian and Tuscan – were to be found both in public buildings and in the houses. The *Doric* order has a column that progressively tapers as it moves upwards to the square capital and has shallow vertical fluting separated by sharp edges and square capitals; the *Ionic* order has a column set on a base,

with numerous flutes separated by fillets and with a pair of volute scrolls on the capital; the *Corinthian* column resembles the Ionic but has a capital decorated with acanthus leaves (a plant with large indented leaves) from which volutes emerge; the *Tuscan* order, with smooth columns and a massive base, was used for rustic buildings. The so-called *Composite order*, a fusion of the Corinthian and the Ionic, also occurs. Roman houses were not all like this though and were often preceded by a shop or tavern depending on the activity of the person living there. Examples of the original 'austere' type of house that was gradually modified in Hellenistic and Roman taste are also found in Pompeii. Patrician houses and villas were enriched with artistic furnish-

◄ *Detail of the fresco depicting the Dionysian Mysteries in the Villa of the Mysteries*

ceding one but the perspective has disappeared and the walls look like ornamental tapestries or carpets. The *Third Style* developed in the Augustan period and seems to have been influenced by Egyptian art when Egypt became a Roman province in 30 BC. The *Fourth Style* is known as "of architectural illusion" or "fantastic" and is almost a return to the *Second Style*, but differs in that the architectural elements are shown in unlikely slender shapes, forming complex and fantastic scenic settings, with bright colors. The *Fourth Style* was fashionable in the second half of the 1st century AD and predominated in Pompeii since it was the most modern and was then 'interrupted' by the eruption. The wall paintings in Pompeii are done in fresco technique, in "tempera" and encaustic. The "fresco" painting was done on a fresh plaster with ground pig-

ments mixed with water, the "tempera" pigments were mixed with glues and gums, with egg yolk and wax; the "encaustic" was painted with colors mixed with wax (the painting was then heated, so that the wax would sink into the colors and fix them). The ground colors were generally red or yellow, but sometimes also black, green or blue. While Roman painting was fond of grand compositions, the domestic rooms of houses, villas and palaces were also frequently decorated with domestic scenes, fantastic views, still lifes, amorous and literary subjects, often with lively portraits. Roman portraiture here had already laid aside

the Hellenistic concept of abstract and impersonal beauty and was often highly individualistic, and passed over into the numerous scenes and folk scenes to be seen everywhere in Pompeii. Mosaic decoration was on a par with painting and was met with everywhere in patrician homes but also, in more modest forms, in the more humble houses. Floors and walls were richly decorated. The various types of mosaic included "*opus alexandrinum*", patterns in black and white on a one-color ground; "*opus tessellatum*" with tiny tesseras arranged in straight lines at the sides; "*opus vermiculatum*" in which the tesseras were arranged in curved lines: "*opus signinum*" which consisted of a random pattern of colored stones; and "*opus sectile*" in which the stones used in a figure composition were cut to the right shape. The vast range of geometric patterns, of figural motifs inspired by the plant and animal world, hunting, battle, sport subjects, etc. present in Pompeian mosaics is not unique in the ancient world, but it is the only example we have in a practically integral form.

▶ *Detail of the painted decoration in the Villa of the Mysteries*

Porta Marina

Normally the entrance to the digs is from Porta Marina, or Marine Gate, so-called because it looks towards the sea. It has two passageways, one for pedestrians, not as steep, the other for animals. The statue of Minerva, patron goddess of the gate, was in the right hand niche. In the times of Augustus and Tiberius, the magnificent suburban Villa of Porta Marina stood on the lower and upper areas of the walls. Destroyed by the earthquake of AD 62 all that can be seen today is a small portion of the portico, the triclinium and living rooms.

Suburban Quarter and Suburban Baths

Proof of the fact that Pompeii, at the time of the eruption, was much more extensive than indicated by the city walls, is a visit to the Suburban quarter, so named because it lies outside the city walls near Porta Marina and close to the better known archaeological area. Initially excavated between 1949 and 1959, more thorough investigation dates to between 1985 and 1989. The area is located on a decidedly scenic artificial terrace outside the walls and stretches out between the sea and one of the bastions of the town. The frequent renovations and expropriations it was subject to before the eruption of AD 79 left dense layers of architectural elements. The core of the Quarter consists of the Suburban Thermae or public baths, dating to the Augustan period, now bringing the number of baths to be seen up to four (the Central Baths, those of the Forum, and the Stabian Baths). Originally laid out on various levels with spacious terraces and with a decidedly scenic aspect, the overall layout of the Baths themselves – at a lower level – is quite unlike the other baths in the city. The Suburban Baths were not divided into distinct sections for men and women, and rather than actual thermae, might have been a "health" center, also in view of the sexual subject matter of the frescoes that decorate the various rooms. The highlight of the visit is the dressing room (*apodyterium*), by some interpreted as a *frigidarium* (cold room), originally frescoed with sixteen erotic scenes (eight now remain) and, below each one, the picture of a drawer where the clothes were placed. Various sexual positions and services are shown, interpreted by scholars

▼ *Porta Marina*

▲ *The Suburban Baths*

▶ *View of the Suburban Quarter*

as a sort of 'catalogue' of what the thermae could offer in the way of paid sexual gratification (probably upstairs, used as a brothel). Other scholars however believe that they are representations of games, widespread in the Greco-Roman world where sexual life was very free. To be noted the picture of the nude poet and, above all, that of Sapphic love between two women, the only one of its kind that has come down to us up to date. All are painted in the *Fourth Style*. Next to the dressing room are a series of rooms, beginning with the *frigidarium* (or unheated pool, with a waterfall in a make-believe grotto and representations of *Mars and Cupids*); then the *tepidarium* (room with warm water); and the *caldarium* (with hot baths). To the South is a large swimming pool (*natatio*), once covered and heated, with double chamber walls, for insulation and to keep the temperature of the water constant.

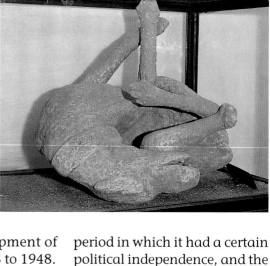

◄►▼ *Casts of people and animals, victims of the eruption*

Antiquarium

Finds from the excavations collected here include weapons, tools, sculpture, architectural fragments and pictorial decoration, vases and plaster casts of the forms left by humans and animals in the solidified ashes. The finest of the works of art found in Pompeii are in the Archaeological Museum in Naples. Since the entire area is currently being reorganized, the Antiquarium is not, at the moment, open to the public.

ENTRANCE – On the walls, decorative sculpture, to be noted the *satyr with a club* and *Eros with the shell*. Wall charts trace the chronological development of excavation from 1748 to 1948.

ROOM ONE – This is dedicated to pre-Samnite Pompeii with finds regarding the early period of the city and the surrounding countryside of the Valle del Sarno. The furnishings are displayed in facing showcases. Showcases 1-6 contain funeral furnishings from the Iron Age, Etruscan-Campanian buccheros (black pottery), bronze jewelry. Showcases 2-5 contain a fine series of architectural terracottas, evidence of the city's earliest past. The fragments of sculpture and painted facing slabs are from the Doric Temple in the Triangular Forum and the Temple of Apollo, friezes, fragments of black-figure and red-figure Greek vases, documenting the customs, cults and the principal monuments of that period.

ROOM TWO – Devoted to Samnite Pompeii, documenting the first period in which it had a certain political independence, and the second in which Greek influence on art, culture and cults is apparent. On the walls, charming figured capitals (the top part of the column). To be noted in the passageway is the *Sphinx* by an Italic-Campanian sculptor. On one side the lovely capital with the figure of a *Maenad crowned by ivy* (the Maenads were women in the retinue of Dionysus) and on the other a *Winged Eros*. On the other side, another capital with the bust of a *Maenad with a tympanon* and that of a *Satyr with pipes*. Along the left and facing walls other magnificent capitals with mythical figures. Of particular interest in case 17 is the Samnite pottery from tombs outside the city. The pediment and altar of the Dionysian shrine, found near the railroad station of Pompei in 1947, are on the back wall.

◀ *Metal fibulas and brooches for clothing*

LIVIA'S ROOM – At the center is the statue of Livia, apparently a cult object, found in the Villa of Mysteries. In the corners *portraits of Cornelius Rufus and Vesonius Primus*, then the small sideboard with the single figured support with *Silenus holding the infant Bacchus in his arms*. Opposite, the *portrait of Marcellus*, nephew of Augustus.

ROOM THREE – Dedicated to Roman Pompeii, this room contains domestic furnishings. At the center is a bronze basin, found in the House of Menander. In the corners bronze figurines of cupids from the House of the Vettii. In case 8 various types of bronze vessels and a series of bone hairpins. Outside the case the lovely *situla* (vessel for transporting liquids) with palmettes and griffins found in the House of Menander. Case 9, a series of ornaments in gold, carved ivory and bone; case 10, statuettes of divinities; case 11, statuette of Pan and domestic furnishings found in the House of Paquius

Proculus and P. Cornelius Teges; case 12, particularly interesting set of women's ornaments in gold and silver. In the passageway, striking casts of human bodies trying desperately to ward off death by suffocation. Note particularly the lovely half-naked body of a young woman lying face down, her head on her arm, and the dog that guarded the House of Vesonius Primus in the last dramatic attempt to free himself from the chain.

ROOM FOUR – This too is dedicated to Roman Pompeii and the collection illustrates specific aspects of business in the city. Case

13 holds the tools of a bronze and silver artisan; 14 the furnishings of people from the sea found on the shores of Pompeii; in case 15, ingredients used in the workshops and shops; in case 16, note the remains of food, bread from the bakery of Modesto. Even though carbonized, it is interesting to see the shape of the loaf of bread about to go into the oven. Case 17 contains various mechanical devices such as locks, hinges, faucets, scales and a fine example of a heater; case 18 contains a series of surgeon's instruments, coins and silver found in the large palaestra and belonging to people who were escaping. At the center of the room, model of a rustic villa with the layout of a wine- growing farm. Back at the entrance to Porta Marina are other plaster casts. Note the cupboard, the wheel, the tree and the mule driver, wrapped in his rough cloak as he tries to defend himself from the rain of fire and ash.

▶ *Altar and pediment of the Dionysian shrine, in room two*

◄ Casts of a wheel and a tree trunk, in the Antiquarium

Basilica

The most important public building in Pompeii was the basilica, used for the administration of justice, and as a place where tradesmen could meet to handle their business. The rectangular area is 24 meters wide and 55 long. Twenty-eight large brick columns divide it into three aisles. At the back is the tribu-

▼ Bird's-eye view of the Forum

Forum

This was the heart of the political, religious and social life of Pompeii. The various public buildings were built around the large rectangular piazza, 38 meters wide and 142 meters long. When the volcano erupted it appears to have had an imposing portico on three sides, with a loggia above supported by smaller columns. The fourth side was occupied by the Temple of Jupiter. On the south, is a portion of trabeation (the part over the columns, consisting of architrave, frieze and cornice) from the Samnite period, while the columns and trabeations on the east and west date to Roman times. A few bases on which statues of worthy citizens once stood are to be seen on the south side of the portico. The much wider base on the west is the so-called orator's tribune.

▲ *View of the remains of the portico that surrounded the area of the Forum*

▼ *The Basilica*

nal (court), a podium with two superposed tiers of columns. Scholars long debated as to just when the building was founded but the discovery of roofing tiles with an Oscan factory mark and the trial digs in the foundations seem to indicate that it may have been built around the year 120 BC, therefore pre-Roman.

▲ *The Basilica from the colonnade of the Tribunal*

Municipal Offices

There are three rooms next to the Basilica used as premises for the municipal offices. This was where the '*duoviri*', the builders and the town council, which met in the largest room, had their headquarters. Originally all these rooms must have been faced with marble slabs.

▲ *Municipal Offices*

Comitium

The Comitium where elections for public offices were held is at the corner with Via dell'Abbondanza. In this large room the electors, divided into "*curiae*", voted on the list of candidates "*proscripta*" before the "*duoviri*" proposed by the electoral assembly.

Building of Eumachia

The building across from the Comitium is the Building of Eumachia, so called from the inscription on the doorway towards Via dell'Abbondanza, which tells us that the it was paid for by the priestess Eumachia, to provide headquarters for the Guild of Fullers, cloth workers, washers

and dyers. Eumachia had dedicated these premises to Concordia Augusta and to Pietas (both personifications of Livia, wife of Augustus). The Fullers Guild was important because its many members had a determining say in the commercial and political activities of the city. Entry is from the side of the Forum. There are two tiers of columns in the portico. The entrance doorway on the facade is framed by a fine marble surround, decorated with acanthus spirals. Upon entering, there is a spacious courtyard with three apses at the back. The central apse contained the statue of the *Empress*. The *cryptoporticus*, a closed portico lit by large windows, runs along behind the wall of the porch. It served as a place for walking and connected to other buildings. The lovely statue of *Eumachia* made by the grateful *Fullones* was found here. It is now in the Archaeological Museum in Naples.

▲ *Via dell'Abbondanza*

▶ *Entrance portal to the Building of Eumachia*

▼ *The portico in front of the Building of Eumachia*

▲ *Temple of Vespasian*

▶ *Marble altar with scene of the Sacrifice of the Bull set in front of the Temple of Vespasian*

Temple of Vespasian

Dedicated to the imperial cult. Note the fine marble *ara* or altar. The scene in relief depicts the sacrificing priest, the *victimarius* (who led the victim to the altar), the *littori*, a flute player and the young ministers of the ceremony. The statue dedicated to the cult was at the back, in an aedicule.

Sacrarium of the Lares

After the famous earthquake of 62 AD, this shrine was built as atonement with a dedication to the tutelary deities of the city (*Lares publici*) and consists of three large architectural wings set around a central square. The side walls with rectangular niches and the large apse-shaped niche at the back were faced with marble and paintings and contained the statues of these gods.

▶ *A few shops in the Macellum, the city market*

Macellum

This complex was built in the imperial age as a covered market, where shops for the sale of food, in particular meat and fish, were located. In front is an elegant portico with marble columns that faced onto the Forum. The moneychangers had their shops under the portico. Inside there is another portico, which collapsed during the earthquake of AD 62, and at the center a circular structure. At the back there were rooms dedicated to the imperial cult and, on the right, the fish market. The Macellum too had been frescoed with mythological themes, with a frieze all around the walls referring to various types of foodstuffs. The statues of *Octavia*, Augustus' sister, and of *Marcellus*, her son, now in the National Museum in Naples, were found in one of the rooms of the Macellum.

▼ *The Macellum with its elegant portico and marble columns*

▲ *The Temple of Jupiter*

Temple of Jupiter

The temple was dedicated to three divinities: Jupiter, Juno and Minerva. It dates to the middle of the 2nd century BC and was the *Capitolium* of Pompeii. It must have been a particularly beautiful and imposing structure with a double staircase and a pronaos (atrium with columns) with Corinthian columns. Inside there was a spacious cella in which an enormous marble head of *Jupiter*, now in the Archaeological Museum of Naples, was found. Partially destroyed by the earthquake, it was being restored when the catastrophic eruption of Vesuvius struck. On either side, triumphal arches dedicated to the imperial family, one perhaps to Tiberius and the other to Germanicus.

Temple of Apollo

On the west side of the Forum is the Temple of Apollo. A niche in the outer wall contains a *tabula ponderaria*, a travertine table showing the standard measures of capacity as compared to those of the Roman system. A bit further on, a row of brick piers indicates the building that was to serve as a grain warehouse.

▼ *Marble altar set opposite the staircase of the Temple of Apollo*

▲ The Temple of Apollo and the sacred enclosure

▲ Copy of the bronze statue of Apollo

In the back, in the left corner, a large latrine, and not far off, two underground rooms that seem to have served as municipal treasury. The Temple already existed in Oscan and Greek times and was dedicated, even then, to this divinity (6th century). In the period of imperial Rome it underwent substantial modifications in line with the more modern architectural and decorative concepts. It had a portico of 48 columns. The *ara* or cult altar was outside in front of the building as usual in Greek and Roman temples. To the left of the staircase a sundial paid for by the *duoviri* L. Sepunius and M. Herennius is set on an Ionic column. After climbing the steps, crowned by a Corinthian colonnade with six columns on the front, one enters the *cella,* the innermost part of the temple where the image of the god was kept. Copies of the bronze statues of *Apollo* and of *Diana* (on the right), now in the Archaeological Museum in Naples, are in front of the portico.

◀ Tepidarium in the Forum Baths

through which hot air went. On the edge of a large basin are written in bronze letters the names of the donors who had it made in the years AD 3-4: "Cneus Melissaeus Aper et M. Staius Rufus". The basin cost 5240 sesterces. Of particular note are the stuccoes in the vault. The Baths, which date to the early period of Roman colonization (80 BC), also have a palaestra.

House of the Tragic Poet

The house takes its name from a mosaic in the tablinum depicting an instructor for actors of the lyric or tragic theater. But the house is even more famous because this is where various

Forum Baths

Although they are not very large, they still give us an idea of the arrangement of such an important public facility and are exceptionally well preserved. The baths are divided into two sections: for men and for women A small corridor leads into the men's dressing room. On the walls, niches for the clothing and seats for those waiting their turn. From here one enters the *frigidarium* (where cold baths were taken in a basin), with stucco decorations on the vaults. Back in the dressing room, on the left, is the entrance to the *tepidarium* (interim room between the hot and cold baths), with a barrel vault decorated with stuccoes and with terra cotta *telamons* (human figures used in architecture to support trabeations and cornices) in the wall niches. Note the *bronze brazier* that served

to heat the room, paid for by Marcus Nigidius Vaccula. From the *tepidarium* one went into the *caldarium* (room for hot bath or sweat bath), with a double wall

▶ Caldarium in the Forum Baths

◄ *Atrium of the House of the Tragic Poet*

triclinium with walls painted with the following mythological subjects: *Venus contemplating a nest of cupids*; *Marsyas and Olympus*; *Theseus abandoning Ariadne* and *Dido and Aeneas*. The *Seasons* are depicted in the compartments at the sides.

Porta Ercolano

Completely rebuilt in the Augustan period when walls and gates were no longer needed for defense, the Herculaneum Gate does indeed resemble an arch of triumph where the central passageway was for wheeled traffic, and the smaller ones at the sides for pedestrians. On the

frescoes of heroic and mythical subject (including the *Sacrifice of Iphigenia*), now in the Archaeological Museum in Naples, were found on the walls of the atrium and the peristyle. It is also famous to the public at large because in his novel "The Last Days of Pompeii" Bulwer Lytton cited it as the house of Glaucus. The dwelling belonged to a citizen of the middle class, who had become wealthy through commercial activities. In the entrance, a mosaic with a watchdog with the words *cave canem* (beware of the dog), in the atrium the marble basin of the *impluvium*, with the various cubicles and staircases that lead to the rooms on the upper floor. The tablinum leads to a small portico with garden, at the back of which is the *lararium* (the place reserved for the *Lares*, the protecting ancestors). To the right of the portico, after the kitchen, the room of the

▲ *Mosaic with the watchdog, located at the entrance to the House of the Tragic Poet*

▶ *Porta Ercolano*

right is the old *"agger"* (earth-work), an embankment for the walls faced with tufa steps that served as buttress but also let the defenders get to the top of the fortification. Remains of 5th century BC Greek walls (second Greek hegemony) were found inside the *agger*.

▼ *Tomb with an aedicule and piers in the Via dei Sepolcri*

Villa of Diomedes

The *Via dei Sepolcri* or Street of Tombs begins outside Porta Ercolano. It was excavated between 1763 and 1838 and is a road around half a kilometer long lined with fine Hellenistic and Roman tombs. Every so often spaces have been left for porticoes or villas, giving the route a unique character, monumental and alive with a variety of architectural forms of patrician tombs. The villa of Diomedes stands at number 24, an imposing suburban dwelling that came to light in 1771-74. It made the headlines thanks to the find in the subterranean portico of eighteen victims of the eruption. Very little is left of the rich decoration, except for the few paintings now in the Archaeological Museum of Naples. Even so a tour of the rooms is worthwhile, for they give us an idea of the layout of a suburban villa that belonged to an affluent family. It seems to have been carefully studied both outside and in to make the most of the lovely views, and is oriented towards the west with floors on two levels. The living quarters are arranged around the atrium-peristyle and move towards the large garden at the lower level. Over the porticoes that surrounded the large *viridarium* (or space for free time and men's sports) was a *solarium* terrace and an *ambulatio* for walking in the open. At the ends were two towers from which one could see the sea. A large gallery (*cryptoporticus*) runs along under the porticoes. It had been turned into a wine cellar in the last years of

◀ *A stretch of the Via dei Sepolcri*

inal *tablinum* then transformed into a room, with the fine miniaturist decoration in Egyptian style on a black-ground wall. Next comes the cubiculum with paintings of the *Second Style*, including the roguish figure of a *dancing Satyr*, and from here, through a small doorway, to the room of the famous painting. Those entering for the first time are spellbound in front of the imposing

◀▼ *The exterior and the atrium-peristyle of the Villa of Diomedes*

the life of Pompeii, with amphorae for wine, in line with the requirements of its last owner, certainly a wine merchant.

Villa of the Mysteries

This imposing quadrilateral building is undoubtedly the most important and best known in Pompeii. The complex interior consists of sixty rooms. The grandiose **Villa of the Mysteries**, which takes its name from the marvelous paintings in one of the rooms that probably represent the *Initiation of the Brides to the Dionysian mysteries*, was discovered in 1902, excavated between 1909-1910 and almost totally restored between 1929 and 1930. The layout of the various rooms provides us with a compendium of all the functional architectural and decorative aspects of life in Pompeii. The entrance, on the west side, leads into a large semicircular exedra with windows, flanked by hanging gardens, followed by the orig-

▶ *Villa of the Mysteries*

▼ *The peristyle of the Villa of the Mysteries*

scene on the wall and the mystic atmosphere, a sense of mysterious meditation even though the subject is far from our ideas of spirituality. Although scholars are still unsure about the actual meaning the prevailing explanation is that it represents the *Initiation rites into the Dionysian mysteries*. The cult of Dionysus was widespread in Campania and Etruria and also reached Rome. Its undoubtedly orgiastic and overt sexual nature brought about severe sanctions against its followers on the part of the Roman Senate. As a result the cult was practiced privately and

▼ *Depiction of the Dionysian Mysteries in the Room of the Large Painting*

▶ *The child Dionysus reads the ritual to the initiate*

by a limited number of initiates. It has been conjectured that these splendid paintings were commissioned from a Campanian artist around the middle of the first century AD by the owner of the villa, a priestess of the Dionysian rite, portrayed as the *matrona* to the right of the entrance. The marvelous composition in the *Second Style* unfolds along the walls, with 29 life-size figures divided into groups, each

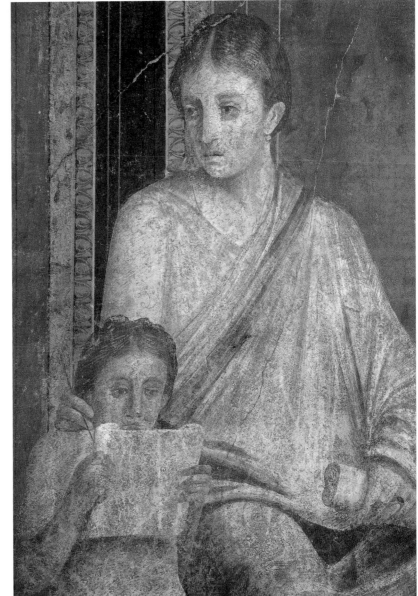

of which represents different sacred or profane moments of the Dionysian myth. The paintings move from left to right: **1)** *The initiation with the reading of the rite by a child;* **2)** *The sacred agape or love-feast, with a maiden bearing a plate with offerings;* **3)** *Silenus playing the lyre and a pastoral scene;* **4)** *A terrified woman fleeing from the sight of a winged demon who*

▶ *Woman administering the purificatory sacrifice*

▲ *Silenus playing the lyre, pastoral scene and terror-stricken initiate fleeing as a companion is flagellated*

◀ *Flagellation of the initiate and dance of the newly initiated*

▼ *Cupid attending the bride and admiring her beauty*

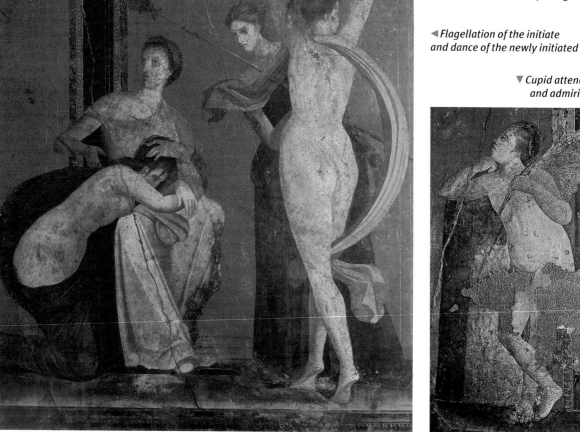

is whipping a companion; **5)** *Silenus with Satyrs*; **6)** *The marriage of Dionysus and Ariadne*; **7)** *Kneeling bacchant raising a cloth that covers the symbol of pleasure and fertility*; **8)** *The woman being flogged* and, not far off, *a dancing nude bacchante in the throes of mysti-* *cal exaltation*; **9)** *Toilette of the bride preparing for initiation into the mystery*; **10)** *Seated cloaked woman*, probably the portrait of the lady of the house and a *Priestess of Dionysus*. The large-figure frieze that moves along in a single level is a monumental composition painted on a dark red ground, with a limited range of colors in which yellows, greens and violet prevail. The figures themselves and the rhythmic arrangement of the groups betray the hand of a great artist and our painter may have reproposed a well-known composition. His pictorial language is rich, his plastic-linear solutions are of such a nature that this can be considered one of the finest masterpieces of Antiquity.

▼ *Detail of the geometric patterns in the pictorial decoration in the Room of the Large Painting*

◄ *The peristyle of the House of Meleager*

which also contains a copy of the *putto with dolphin* (the original is in the Archaeological Museum in Naples).

House of the Faun

From the temple of the Goddess Fortuna, turning right into the street by the same name, at no. 2-5 is the House of the Faun. A beautiful bronze of a *dancing faun*, after which the house is named, was found in the impluvium. The statue there now is a copy of the original in the Archaeological Museum of Naples. This is one of the largest and most sumptuous dwellings

House of Meleager

A beautiful elegant house of the Samnite period, with *Fourth Style* decoration. Of particular note is the lovely peristyle with a large garden basin in the center and with statuettes. There are three large rooms to the right of the peristyle. The one in the center has a Greek style colonnade and served as a luxurious reception room (*oecus*). The imposing triclinium beyond was once richly decorated.

House of the Great Fountain

Adjacent to the House of the Small Fountain, this house too has a marvelous mosaic fountain at the back of the tablinum. Traces of landscapes with villas and houses in the countryside and on the sea are still visible on the walls of the Nymphaeum

► *The mosaic fountain in the House of the Great Fountain*

▲ Atrium of the House of the Faun

▲ Dancing faun, from the House of the Faun, now in the Archaeological Museum of Naples

of Samnite period (2nd century BC) but every architectural element reveals Greek and Italic influences. Precious mosaics, now in the Archaeological Museum, come from this house, including the famous *Battle of Alexander*. On the threshold, the word *"Have"* (hail) greets the visitor. In the vestibule the floor is in colored marble and the polychrome walls represent a marble facing. Above are two *larari* in stucco. Then comes the imposing atrium, with fine decorations on the walls, leading into the wings with floors once decorated with mosaics. The triclinium rooms are on either side of the tablinum, after which comes the small tetrastyle atrium, the first peristyle composed of twenty-eight Ionic columns with a large basin with fountain at the center. At the back, the exedra, on the floor of which was the famous *Alexander mosaic*, with other triclinium rooms on either side. Domestic rooms (kitchen, bath and a stable) are to the right of the peristyle. A corridor leads to another large peristyle with garden.

House of the Labyrinth

Another example of Samnite style, with two atriums of which the most important one has four columns (tetrastyle). At the back of the peristyle are the formal reception rooms. The one in the middle is particularly sumptuous. The peristyle has an internal colonnade (*"hoecus corinthius"*) and lovely *Second Style* decorations on the walls. They resemble those of the Villa of Mysteries so closely that they might be by the same painter. A

▲ *Painted architectural structures in the oecus of the House of the Labyrinth*

▼ *The peristyle and the garden of the House of the Vettii*

House of the Vettii

The brothers Aulus Vettius Restitutus and Aulus Vettius Conviva, affluent merchants, owned this fine home. In building their wonderful house however they did all they could to forget their merchant origins. They felt themselves true gentlemen and wanted to be thought of as such. Here we have a truly complete idea of what the Roman house of a member of the well-to-do class in Pompeii was like, all the more considering that it was almost completely restored after the disastrous earthquake of AD 62. In addition to the layout of the rooms, the House of the Vettii is universally known because of its wealth of wall decorations in the *Fourth Style*. The carefully conducted archaeological dig has made it possible to reconstruct the entire original structure, roofing it over and restoring it, providing the visitor with

mosaic depicting *Theseus and the Minotaur in the Labyrinth* is set into the floor of the next room. The large peristyle, much of which is still intact, is also of interest.

▲ *The lararium in the House of the Vettii*

heads of the *Medusa* and of *Silenus*. To the right of the main atrium, a small atrium with a *lararium*. The *Genius* head of the family is shown between two *Lari* while a serpent below approaches the altar set with funeral offerings. The cook's room, and in a small courtyard, the kitchen with a hearth with tripod and a bronze boiler. Facing the kitchen is a small room with erotic pictures. From here to the women's quarter (*gynaeceum*) with a triclinium and a charming small portico. Out into the large peristyle that encloses a lovely garden with flowerbeds, statuettes in bronze and marble, and basins with gurgling water. This garden is unique in that it was created as originally planned after the excavations had unearthed the ancient water pipes. From the large triclinium room, where joyful *symposia* or Greek-style drinking par-

a real sense of intimate family life. A depiction of *Priapus*, god of fertility, greets the eye upon entering the vestibule. The superstitious Vettii had it painted to protect themselves from the evil eye those envious of their prosperity might cast on them. Through the *fauces*, one enters the atrium with the *impluvium* at the center to collect rain from the roof. At the sides two safes where money and silver were kept are set on piers with figures of cupids and maidens on the bases. In the small room to the left of the entrance, a frieze with fish in a fishpond, and below, two small pictures: *Ariadne abandoned* and *Hero and Leander*. In the much larger next room are other paintings: *Cyparissus*; *Pan and Eros wrestling*. Above: *Jupiter enthroned* and *Leda and Danae*. The ala on the left has a painted picture of a *Cockfight*, while the one on the right has small but expressive medallions with the

▶ *Priapus, god of fertility, fresco in the vestibule of the House of the Vettii*

▲ *Paintings in the oecus of the House of the Vettii*

◄ *The infant Hercules strangling the serpents, in the oecus of the House of the Vettii*

ties were held, the peristyle and the garden could be seen in all their beauty. This room has fine decoration along the red-ground walls, framed by pilasters with black bands. Every frame must have had a panel painting at the center, but nothing remains, while in the lower zone, a frieze runs along the dado showing *Cupids* engaged in various occupations. From right to left: *Cupids* throwing stones at a target, others making garlands and buy-ing flowers, those preparing and selling perfumed oils, the chariot race, *Cupid* goldsmiths and metal workers, those who dye cloth, who celebrate the Vestal Virgins, vintners, the triumph of Bacchus and those selling wine. Below the frieze with *Cupids*, panels with *flower-bearing Psychai*. The central frames of the long walls contain panels with mythological subjects. On the right wall: *Agamemnon about to kill the sacred hind* and *Apollo defeating the Python*. On the left wall: *Orestes and Pylades before Thoas and Iphigenia*. In the side panels, pairs of mythical lovers: *Perseus and*

▲ *Cyparissus unhappy because he has killed the deer beloved by Apollo, fresco in the oecus of the House of the Vettii*

Andromeda, Dionysus and Ariadne, Apollo and Daphne, Poseidon and Amymone. After this comes the smaller triclinium with fine wall paintings: on the left: *Daedalus showing Pasiphae the wooden cow*, opposite, *Ixion, with Hera present, is bound by Zeus on the wheel made by Hephaestus*; on the right: *Dionysus and the sleeping Ariadne*. On the other side of the atrium, in the larger room, from the left: the *Infant Hercules strangling the serpents*; opposite, *Pentheus torn to pieces by the Bacchantes*, right; *Amphion and Zethus bind Dirce to a bull*.

the left. *Paris and Helen in Sparta* are depicted on the back wall of the tablinum. The atrium leads to the elegant peristyle, with a higher western side due to the irregular terrain. This solution resulted in a fine scenic effect. So-called *oscilla*, marble disks with various figures, hang between the columns. In the south wing, a finely carved marble fragment with a *Silenus* and other fragments. The triclinium is between the atrium and the peristyle, with *Third Style* paintings on the walls. On the left: *Thetis in Vulcan's smithy*; on the back side: *Jason wearing a single sandal before Pelias*; right: *Achilles, Briseis and Patrocles in the tent*. At the center of the west portico, a large triclinium with a small room on either side. Note the mural paintings of *Diana and Actaeon, Leda, Venus fishing*, in the one on the right. In the north portico, next to a large decorated room, is the cubicle with the *cupids*.

The **House of the Golden Cupids** opens onto Via del Vesuvio, with deep ruts in the paving where wagons continuously passed. On the left, at the back,

House of the Golden Cupids

The patrician home of Cneo Poppaeus Habitus, named after the decoration in the matrimonial cubicle, with Cupids in gold leaf set onto small glass disks,

reflects the dwellings of the patrician class in the period of Nero. After the entrance, in the atrium, the cubicle on the right has a floor with *Leda and the swan* and *Narcissus at the spring*, while there is a *Flying Mercury* in the one on

▼ *Detail of the frieze with scenes of Cupids, in the large triclinium of the House of the Vettii*

in the imperial period. The impression on entering is that of a grandiose dignity, conferred by the imposing tetrastyle atrium, supported by gigantic Corinthian columns and with decorations in the *Second Style*. Next comes the peristyle with the most luxurious rooms on the south. Note the impressive room with four columns painted in porphyry red supporting the vault, and with walls painted with architectural structures of the *Second Style*. Cubicles with the same decoration and a room with black walls are in the ambulacrum. This is also where the premises of a private bath with *caldarium* and *tepidarium* are to be found, with the basin for cold baths in the garden.

▲ *The garden with portico in the peristyle of the House of the Golden Cupids*

▶ *The tetrastyle oecus with vaulting in the House of the Silver Wedding*

is the **Porta Vesuvio**, or Vesuvius Gate, one of the most important of the city, damaged in the earthquake and under restoration when Vesuvius erupted. Next to it, the building for the water reservoir from a branch of the aqueduct of the Serino.

House of the Silver Wedding

The house was excavated in 1893, the year in which the king and queen of Italy celebrated their silver wedding, hence the name. This beautiful patrician dwelling dates to the Samnite period, but it was renovated in its structure and decorations

▲ *The Marriage of Venus and Mars and the Triumph of Bacchus, small panels in the tablinum of the House of M. Lucretius Fronto*

House of M. Lucretius Fronto

A small house of the imperial period, it has fine well-executed painting in the *Third Style*.

In the tablinum, in addition to panels with landscapes, are two small paintings: the *Marriage of Venus and Mars* and the *Triumphal Procession of Bacchus*. In the large

triclinium: *Neoptolemus killed by Orestes in Delphi*. To the right of the tablinum, in a room: *Narcissus at the spring* and *Pero nursing her old father Micon*. In a cubicle to the right of the atrium: *Theseus and Ariadne* and the *Toilette of Venus*. On the back wall the garden has a fine decoration with *Scenes of the hunt*.

House of Obellius Firmus

A fine house of Samnite times with a double atrium and a double entrance. The larger atrium is tetrastyle. To be noted in the impluvium is a charming statuette of a *Satyr* (the original is in the Archaeological Museum of Naples). On his right, the lararium and a safe (*arca*). At the back of the peristyle a large room and a cubicle decorated with paintings in the *Second Style*.

House of the Centennial

Since it was discovered in 1879, eighteen hundred years af-

◀ *The tetrastyle atrium of the House of Obellius Firmus*

◀ *Hermaphrodite, Silenus and Orestes, fresco in one of the rooms of the House of the Centennial*

the back of the peristyle is a small courtyard with an enchanting fountain decorated with paintings depicting scenes of the hunt, views of gardens and a fishpond. On the west side, through a narrow corridor, one arrives at apartments with a lararium in the atrium. The painting once there (now in the Archaeological Museum in Naples) depicted *Bacchus at the foot of a wooded mountain with vines*, which has been identified as Vesuvius before the eruption. Continuing, are a bath and a few rooms. One, with a black ground, has three small pictures: *Theseus and the Minotaur*; *Hermaphrodite, Silenus and Orestes*; *Pylades and Iphigenia*. then comes a room decorated with erotic scenes.

ter the famous eruption, it was called House of the Centennial. The building consisted of three dwellings and was transformed in the imperial period, before and after the earthquake of 62. To be noted the spacious Tuscan atrium, its mosaic floor and the impluvium. The walls are decorated with *Fourth Style* paintings of theater subjects. On either side of the tablinum, a small room with charming decorative motifs. Next comes the peristyle, with yellow panels on the walls containing the emblems of *Juno, Apollo* and *Minerva*. The pool in the garden once held the charming bronze of a *Satyr with a wineskin* (now in the Archaeological Museum of Naples). At

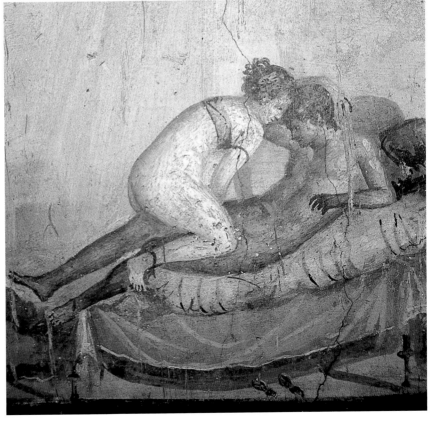

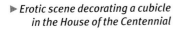
▶ *Erotic scene decorating a cubicle in the House of the Centennial*

◄ *A millstone in Modesto's Bakery, one of the most interesting and best-preserved bakeries in Pompeii*

Central Baths

The central Baths are the most up to date expression of a Roman bath complex, since they were built after 62 in accordance with the dictates of the most exacting taste of the times. They were however never finished. They cover the area of an entire *insula,* or city block, and on the north and east had numerous shops. The main entrance was on Via Stabiana and leads immediately to a large palaestra with opposite, in the back, the *natatio*, or swimming pool. On the south is the lavatory with the dressing rooms. On the east side is another large dressing room,

Modesto's Bakery

The number of bakeries in Pompeii seems to indicate that making bread was one of the most florid trades in the city. It can also be supposed that part of the product was sent to the surrounding towns and resold. The bakery, or *pistrinum*, of Modesto is one of the most interesting and best preserved. In front of the oven four large millstones in lava stone used to grind the wheat to flour can still be seen. Some of the eighty loaves found carbonized in the oven are in the Antiquarium.

► *Via Stabiana with the entrance to the Central Baths*

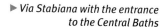

▶ *The hanging garden of the House of Marcus Lucretius*

the *tepidarium* and the *laconicum*, a room for sweat baths, circular in shape with a dome. Then comes the *caldarium*, which has apsed and rectangular niches set into the walls with large windows that let in light. This, together with the *laconicum*, is another element that shows us the difference in construction and layout with respect to the earlier Forum Baths.

House of Marcus Lucretius

This house belonged to Marcus Lucretius, an important citizen of Pompeii, a *decurion* (commander of one *decuria* of the Roman cavalry) and priest of Mars. His residence reflected his dignity. In the atrium, on the right, the lararium, opposite a spacious tablinum, and behind this, in a higher position, is the garden with a fine fountain. Marble herms (square stone pillars surmounted by a bust or head) and charming statuettes of *Silenus with a wineskin*, *Satyrs*, *Pan*, *Cupid riding a dolphin* and *figures of animals* are set in the niche and in the flowerbeds. The house had beautiful paintings in the *Fourth Style*, now detached and in the Archaeological Museum in Naples. Those still in the tablinum depict the *Triumph of Bacchus*, *followed by a Satyr and a Victory*.

Stabian Baths

The entrance is from Via dell'Abbondanza. These baths date to the period of the republican colony and were renovated more than once, in particular the decoration that belongs to the imperial period. Restoration was begun after the earthquake of 62, but was interrupted by the eruption. Entering, one is in the large palaestra with plastered

◀ *The portico of the palaestra of the Stabian Baths*

▲ *Detail of the columns in the palaestra of the Stabian Baths*

◄ *The dressing room, apodyterium, with benches and shelving for clothing*

columns on three sides. Immediately to the right, the vestibule of the men's section with a figured stucco decoration. Then comes the dressing room with a coffered vault in stucco with trophies of weapons and other figures, and from here those who wished to go to the *frigidarium* entered by returning to the vestibule, a circular room with a dome, and painted decoration depicting marine fauna on the walls and niches. Back in the

◄ *The caldarium, with decorations in stucco, of the Stabian Baths*

six Ionic columns (only four can be seen, preceded by a public fountain). A portico of the Ionic order with 95 columns runs along three sides. In front of the entrance is the base on which the statue of the nephew of the Emperor Augustus, Marcus Claudius Marcellus, once stood. Almost at the center is what remains of a **Doric Temple** dedicated to the cult of Hercules and Minerva, from the period in which Pompeii was under Etruscan hegemony.

Samnite Palaestra

This small rectangular space has a Doric colonnade along three sides. Built in the Samnite period by the quaestor Vibius Vinicius, it was used for sport contests by Pompeian youths of patrician and well-to-do families. Votive crowns that the winners offered to the god Mercury, patron of sport games, were placed on the altar table.

dressing room, at the back on the left, is the entrance to the *tepidarium* that was heated with hot air from a space beneath the floor. From there on to the apsed room with a tub for hot baths, the *caldarium*. Note the fine stucco frieze that runs along the walls. For the women's section one must backtrack to the palaestra. Just outside the vestibule turn to the right and almost at the back of the colonnade a passageway leads to the dressing room, the *tepidarium* and the *caldarium*. Back in the palaestra, the oldest part of the baths, composed of various small rooms reached from the Vicolo del Lupanare, is on the north side. The west side belongs to the last period of Pompeii. Note the open-air swimming pool with rooms for changing and for anointing with oil and sand along the sides. These

served for those who practiced sports such as wrestling, boxing, gymnastics.

Triangular Forum

Named for its geometric shape, Greek influence is much more notable here than elsewhere. Access to the forum is through the lovely *propylaea* (monumental columned porch) with

► *Entrance to the Triangular Forum*

plans. The architect skillfully exploited a natural space the hillside offered where he built a *cavea maxima*, that is the tiers reserved for the spectators.

Only a few lower tiers remain of the cavea, which could hold five thousand people. Opposite the cavea is the stage with niches

◄ *The cavea and the stage of the Large Theater*

▼ *The tufa Telamon at the end of the parapet in the Small Theater*

Large Theater

This lovely theater was built according to the dictates of Hellenistic architecture, in the period between 200-150 BC and enlarged by the architect M. Artorius in the Augustan age, in line with specifically Roman

▲ *The cavea and the stage of the Small Theater*

▲ *The quadriporticus of the Gladiators' Barracks*

and aedicules, before which there was room for the orchestra. At present classic theater performances are given here during the tourist season.

Small Theater (Odeion)

This covered theater was used particularly for musical performances and prose. It was built between 80 and 75 BC by the magistrates C. Quintius Valgus and Marcus Porcius and could hold no more than a thousand spectators. The *cavea maxima* is well preserved, and is one of the finest examples of ancient theater architecture.

Gladiators' Barracks

This imposing quadriporticus was not originally for the gladiators, but was a meeting place for the many spectators that crowded into the Large Theater. Here, in the pauses between spectacles, they could walk and exchange opinions on what they had seen. In the Neronian pe-

riod it was transformed into a barracks for the gladiators who took part in the spectacles and who lived here in training for the gladiator games. The rooms for their families were on two floors at the outer edges of the quadriporticus The interesting pieces of fine gladiatorial equipment now in the Archaeological Museum in Naples come from here.

Temple of Isis

Dating to the pre-Roman period, this temple was rebuilt after the earthquake of 62 by Numerius Popidius Ampliatus in the name of his son Numerius Popidius Celsinus. Enclosed by tall walls, it still has its original structure. Next to the staircase is a large altar, the shrine on a tall podium with a *pronaos* and a small rectangular cella. A small temple with decorations in stucco is in the southeast corner of the peristyle. It led to a tiny subterranean cave where the water of the Nile was kept. The followers of Isis met in a spacious room behind the temple

▲ *The Temple of Isis*

while the priests' quarters are nearby.

Fullonica Stephani (Laundry)

This is one of the largest establishments of the cloth workers or *fullones* found so far and is still another example of a dwelling house turned into workshop. Dirty clothes arrived at the back of the fullery, except for the delicate ones, which were treated in the old atrium where the impluvium had been transformed into a tub and was equipped for its new function. The clothes were hung to dry in the sun on the terrace above. The clean clothes were sorted in the former triclinium and went into the former "*oecus*" where they were pressed and mended. It was also here, the largest room,

▲ *Room inside the Fullonica Stephani or Laundry*

that the clothes were delivered or, if produced by the firm, shown and sold to the clients.

House of the Cryptoporticus

What makes this house so interesting is the beautiful cryptoporticus at the bottom of a flight of steps. There are traces of *Second Style* decoration. The barrel vault is faced with stucco and decorated with floral motifs, with a large frieze with *Scenes from the Iliad* all around. Showcases contain plaster casts of many of the inhabitants who sought refuge in the cryptoporticus but who died of asphyxiation. In the triclinium, *Second Style* decorations with caryatids, small pictures and still lifes.

House of Menander

One of the loveliest and most interesting houses in Pompeii, owned by the patrician Quin-

◄ *Stuccoes and paintings in the oecus of the House of the Cryptoporticus*

▲ *The peristyle of the House of Menander*

ridor leads to the kitchen and cellars and it is in one of the latter that the silver was found.

House of Paquius Proculus

The owner was an influential figure, and his name appears in various election programs. In the vestibule, the figure of a chained dog. Tablinum and triclinium are decorated with fine mosaics. There are skeletons of seven children who took refuge here from the eruption in an exedra on the north side of the peristyle. The garden was equipped for open-air dining. A loggia on the upper floor overlooked the portico. The portrait of *Paquius Proculus and his wife*, well known for the excep-

tus Poppaeus, relative of Nero's second wife, Poppaea Sabina, it takes its name from the painted portrait of the Greek poet Menander. In 1930 a cache in silver composed of 115 pieces now in the Archaeological Museum in Naples was found here. The house is once more open to the public after recent restoration.

In the atrium note the *Fourth Style* paintings, the lararium in the form of a small temple, the exedra on the left with paintings of mythical subjects: *Trojan Horse, Death of Laocoon; Menelaos and Helen meeting in Priam's Palace*. Then, after the tablinum, come the imposing peristyle with black and red columns, the triclinium on the east with a large jar on either side. On the south, a row of apse-shaped and rectangular exedrae or alcoves with the *portrait of Menander* and *scenes of the hunt*; on the west side a fine bath with *caldarium*, decorated with mosaics and paintings. On coming out of the bath, a cor-

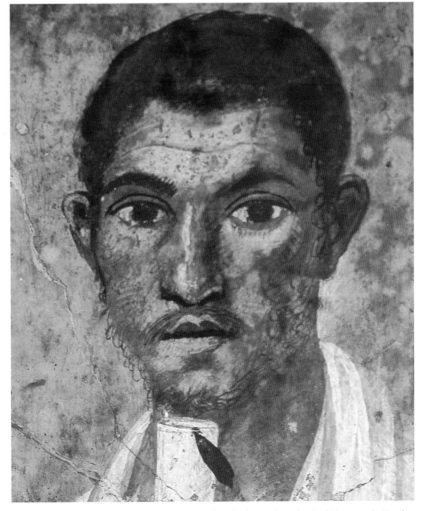

▲ *Portrait of Paquius Proculus, in the Archaeological Museum in Naples*

◄ *The open triclinium in the House of the Ephebus*

tional vitality of the painting, was found here and taken to the National Museum in Naples.

House of the Ephebus

T he house is named after the bronze statue of the *Ephebus*, now in the Archaeological Museum in Naples, that was found here. The large premises consist of the union of three apartments. Note particularly the triclinium

▲ *The garden with a canal cutting through it, House of Loreius Tiburtinus*

▲ *The peristyle of the House of Venus*

with its couches and the marble intarsia of the floor. The lararium and a painting with *Mars and Venus* are in the garden.

House of Loreius Tiburtinus

Of particular note in this patrician home is the large portal with bronze bosses, leading to the rectangular atrium. The surrounding rooms are all finely decorated with red, white and yellow walls. Beyond the atrium and peristyle is the long porticoed loggia with a pergola and at the center a small tetrastyle temple, then the canal bordered by marble statuettes of animals and muses. At the back of the canal is the triclinium room with two signed paintings ("*Lucius pinxit*") depicting *Narcissus* and *Pyramus and Thisbe*. On another

side of the loggia, another triclinium room decorated with a frieze showing *Scenes from the Iliad* and the *Labors of Hercules*. On the west side a white ground cubicle gives us one of the most perfect examples of *Fourth Style* painting. To be noted among the various figures and medallions is that of the *priest of Isis*, with the inscription "*amplus alumnus Tiburs*", which may very well be the portrait of one of the members of this patrician family.

House of the Marine Venus

Uncovered in 1952, this house takes its name from a monumental painting on the back wall of the garden depicting *Marine Venus escorted by Cupids*. It may not be a masterpiece but the artist did succeed in obtain-

▲ *Mars, detail of the painting on the back wall of the garden of the House of the Marine Venus*

ing a certain scenic and color effect. To the left is the image of *Mars*. In the atrium, on the right side, a black-ground cubicle with a medallion of a *young cithara player* and a *still life*.

▲ The portico and the fishpond in the House of Julia Felix

▲ Terracotta statue of Pittacos,
the Greek sage, located in the garden
of the House of Julia Felix

Villa of Julia Felix

This house takes up an entire city block and was completely uncovered in 1952-53 after initially being excavated between 1755-57. A rental notice painted on an entrance door gave us the name of the owner (the notice is in the Archaeological Museum in Naples). There are three parts to the premises: the owner's dwelling on Via dell'Abbondanza and, on the same street, a public bath and a rental area with a tavern and shops. In the eighteenth century nine figures of Apollo and the Muses were removed from the northeast corner of a room and are now in the Louvre in Paris. The garden with a portico and fishpond (*euripus*), decorated with marble and terracotta sculpture, must have been lovely. Note particularly the terracotta statue of the Greek sage *Pittacos*. Under the portico, on the west, the triclinium, once decorated with a fine *still life* frieze now in the Archaeological Museum in Naples. The private baths had the canonical layout, with dressing room, rectangular *frigidarium*, *tepidarium* and a domed *laconicum* for the sweat baths.

▲ *Porta di Nocera*

▲ *Casts of victims of the eruption in the Garden of the Fugitives*

Garden of the Fugitives and Porta di Nocera

The imprints left in the ashes of thirteen victims of the eruption – adults and children (hence the name of the space) – were discovered in 1961 behind the portico of a rustic house with vegetable garden. Backtracking to be noted is the **Porta di Nocera**, or Nucerian Gate, a pre-Roman structure restored in Roman times. The casts of the victims found in the area have been placed outside the gate, along the fortification wall. At the beginning of Via di Nocera, ex-cavations brought to light the **Necropolis** with an interesting group of tombs, including that of Eumachia who had the building for the Fullers Guild built in the Forum, and numerous others of magistrates and military tribunes.

Amphitheater

Built in 80 BC for the same magistrates who built the Small Theater, it can be considered the oldest amphitheater that has come down to us. The imposing elliptical circuit with its great rows of tiers seated twelve thousand spectators. It measured 135 by 104 meters. At the top of the *summa cavea* are large stone rings that supported the armature for the *velarium*, an awning that protected the spectators from the sun and rain. There are no subterranean structures.

▼ *The exterior of the Amphitheater*

◀ The interior of the Amphitheater

The Large Palaestra

Excavated between 1936 and 1951, this quadrilateral area of 130 by 140 meters has porticoes on three sides, with a large swimming pool (*natatio*) in the center. This is where the young people of Pompeii gathered to train for the gymnastic games and their favorite sports. The swimming pool was once surrounded by two rows of large plane trees to provide shade in the heat of summer. Casts of their roots can be seen.

▼ The Large Palaestra

New Pompei

The inhabited center of new Pompei begins outside the excavations. The town occupies a territory, known as **Campo Pompeiano**, that was populated even after the famous eruption of AD 79. A church dedicated to the Savior was built and a castle that belonged to the Caracciolo, all part of a patrician feud that passed from one lord to another depending on the political events of the Kingdom of Naples. In 1873 a lawyer, Bartolo Longo (1841-1926), a pious and charitable man, promoted devotion among the inhabitants to the Holy Rosary and founded the Shrine of Our Lady of the Rosary around which, with the help of the faithful, he built hospices and orphanages. The Shrine soon became a center of a fervid religious life, famous for its cult of the Virgin. Pilgrimages come here from all parts of Italy, mostly in summer and autumn (to be noted is that one of the principal Roman Catholic churches in

▼ ▶ Shrine of Our Lady of the Rosary and interior

◀ *The high altar with the venerated image of Our Lady*

chrome effect: in the dome, frescoes, and on the walls, mosaics. In the center the high altar has the venerated image of *Our Lady of the Rosary* framed by a myriad of precious stones. Access to the treasury is in the left aisle. It contains particularly fine religious and votive objects, a panel painting of *Saint Paul* attributed to Fra Bartolomeo, a *candleholder for the Paschal candle* by Vincenzo Ierace, portraits of the popes, benefactors and founders.

The piazza of the Shrine communicates with that of the Town Hall, on the left of which is the Via Sacra, with the **Terme Fonte Salutare**, a spa where mud and baths are used to treat rheumatism, aesthemia, breakdowns and metabolism diseases.

New York is dedicated to the Our Lady of Pompei, evidence of how extensive this worship is). The imposing building of the Shrine on the main square was begun on May 8, 1876 to designs by the architect Antonio Cua and was consecrated on May 7, 1891. Between 1933-39 it was enlarged on designs of the engineer Monsignor Spirito Chiappetta. The facade by Giovanni Rispoli has two tiers of orders: Ionic below and Corinthian above. At the center is the papal loggia (the Shrine enjoys the title of papal basilica and the archbishop rector is named by the pope). Above is the marble statue of *Our Lady of the Rosary* by the sculptor Gaetano Chiaramonte. The large *bell tower* to the left of the facade was built between 1912 and 1925 to designs by the architect Aris-

tide Leonori. It is 80 meters high and consists of five levels with a fine bronze door. There are four bronze *angels* on the corners of the third level and the belfry has eleven bells. The gigantic statue of the *Sacred Heart of Jesus*, in Carrara marble and 6 meters high, is in the niche on the fourth level while at the top a large cross surmounts the terrace. A marvelous panorama of old Pompeii and the new city, of Vesuvius, the sea, the Sarno valley and the mountains can be had from here (elevator). The church is Latin-cross in plan with a nave and side aisles. Precious marbles have been profusely used everywhere, with a luminous poly-

▶ *Monument to Bartolo Longo*

HERCULANEUM

Ancient Herculaneum was a small peaceful town on the far slopes of Mt. Vesuvius, barely four miles from Neapolis (Naples). Little is known of its origins: Dionysus of Halicarnassus says it was founded by Hercules and therefore, implications apart, considered it to be of Greek origin, while Strabo (not however thought to be particularly reliable) believed it was an Oscan city subsequently conquered by the Etruscans and the Pelasgians (a people who wandered around the Mediterranean) and, then, by the Samnites. At least as early as the 6th century BC, it was surely under Greek dominion, for which there is evidence throughout Campania, and by the late 5th century BC it passed under the Samnites. Just what role Herculaneum played in the Second Samnite War against the Romans is not clear. We do however know that it participated in the Social War, and

in 89 BC fell to Titus Didius, a lieutenant of Sulla, and became a Roman municipium. Up to early imperial times life seems to have been rather uneventful, and Herculaneum remained a small cultured provincial center, favored by its climate and a charming landscape, a favorite resort for affluent Romans and even for members of the Imperial family. Seriously damaged in the earthquake of AD 62, the city was cancelled from the face of the earth by the eruption of Vesuvius

(AD 79) that covered it with a mass of rain-swept mud, ashes and other eruptive materials that penetrated every crack and solidified in a hard compact layer 15-20 meters thick (much higher than in Pompeii). The circumstances that led to the burial of Herculaneum make excavation a particularly arduous task, yet they also permitted highly perishable materials such as wood, cloth, papyri and foodstuffs, sealed in by the mud, to be preserved. Centuries after it was buried and after the modern city of Resina sprang up on part of its territory, the rediscovery of Herculaneum took place almost by chance in the early 18th century when the Austrian prince D'Elboeuf, who owned a villa in Por-

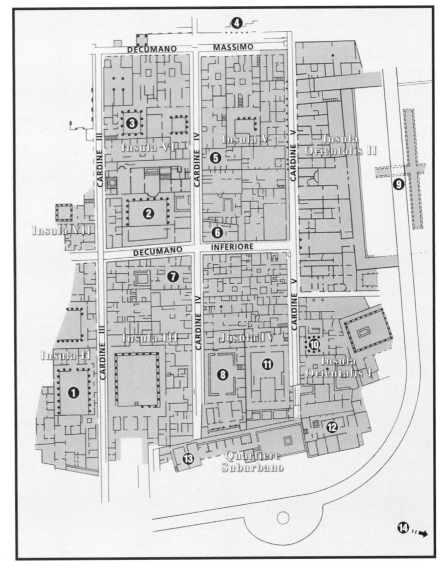

tici, learned that an old building decorated with marble had been intercepted in digging a well in the kitchen garden of the Alcantarini Friars. What had been struck was the theater of Herculaneum and *L'Elboeuf* continued his explorations, removing statues, facing marble, columns, inscriptions and bronzes to the Royal Villa of Portici.

The first regular excavation campaign was carried out between 1738

▲ *View of Cardo III; compared with the streets of Pompeii, those of Herculaneum showed fewer signs of wagon traffic, had no blocks for pedestrian crossings and had more porticoed streets*

▲ *The southwest quarter of Herculaneum*

and 1765, sponsored by Charles of Bourbon and initially directed by Alcubierre (assisted by Karl Weber) and then by Francesco La Vega. Conditions were extremely trying and consisted of tunnels that were closed once the works of art had been removed. Several temples, the so-called Basilica and the Villa of the Papyri were reached. Fortunately Karl Weber began to draw up a plan on the basis of the discoveries. It was completed by Francesco La Vega and was of inestimable importance for subsequent studies.

From 1828 to 1835 and from 1869 to 1875 the results of the excavations, finally above ground, were rather modest. Resumed in 1927 by Amedeo Maiuri, they are still in progress. The finds have demonstrated that, as in Pompeii, not all the inhabitants of Herculaneum managed to save themselves (as was initially thought since no victims had been found in the urban area). Numerous skeletons have been found in the belt of land that separated the city from the sea, men, women and children of all social classes, caught in the river of mud as they attempted to flee, some with jewelry and other objects.

The Herculaneum we see today is only the part closest to the sea, while portions of the Forum, the temples, many houses and the necropoli still lie buried beneath the modern residential center of Resina. The spa-cious city blocks are separated by streets that are called Cardines, which have been numbered to make identification easier.

▶ *Portrait bust in wood, in the Antiquarium, that bears witness to the state of preservation of perishable materials after they were buried in Herculaneum*

A large *labrum* shaped basin in cipollino marble is still in its place in the apse of the back wall, while little remains of the small rectangular basin nearby. The *frigidarium*, rather small in size, has a dome painted with marine creatures on a grayish-light blue background . The *tepidarium* has an interesting mosaic floor, with

▼ *The women's apodyterium in the Central Baths, with the splendid floor mosaic depicting a triton and marine creatures*

▲ *The peristyle of the House of Argos*

House of Argos

A scene with *Io and Argos*, formerly painted on a wall of the large peristyle room, no longer extant, gave its name to the house. It must have been one of the noblest dwellings in Herculaneum, with a spacious garden surrounded by a splendid peristyle with columns and piers.

Central Baths

Consisting, as was usual for this type of building, of two parts, one for men and the other for women (*gynaeceum*), it dated to the Augustan period but was remodeled later. Entrance to the men's section is from Cardo III, where a long corridor leads into the palaestra with porticoes on three sides, used not only for gymnastic exercises but also as a meeting place or "waiting room". From here to the dressing room (*apodyterium*) with barrel vault, seats on three sides and closets for hanging up clothes.

▲ *The women's tepidarium with a labyrinth-pattern in mosaic on the floor*

phins, an *octopus* and a *squid*. The mosaic floor of the *tepidarium* with its geometric pattern is also interesting. The *caldarium* was spacious with an oculus at the top of the vault letting in light.

House of the Tuscan Colonnade

Originally built in the Samnite period with large blocks of tufa, it was later restored. After the earthquake of AD 62 it must in part have lost its patrician nature, for two rooms overlooking the public street were converted into shops. The house is distinguished by its splendid peristyle with a majestic Tuscan colonnade, on which the triclinium, a few official rooms and the patrician lodgings open. The rooms were decorated in two different periods, with paintings both of the *Third* and *Fourth Style*. A cache of gold coins (around 1400 sesterces) was found in the house, probably hidden by the wealthy owner shortly before leaving.

a triton surrounded by four dolphins. A door leads into the large *caldarium*, with a tub for hot water baths and with the *labrum* for cold water ablutions.

Smaller and more sober, but better preserved, are the women's baths, with entrance on Cardo IV: a doorway leads into a large hall that served as vestibule, but undoubtedly also as a waiting room. From here a small narrow vestibule led to the *apodyterium* with a floor mosaic depicting a *triton* carrying a steering rudder, surrounded by a *cupid,* four *dol-*

▲ *The garden and peristyle of the House of the Tuscan Colonnade*

▲ *The atrium of the House of the Tuscan Colonnade*

Forum

The Decumanus Maximus cut through the Forum of Herculaneum. The street was unusually wide, 12-14 meters, and thus comprised the platea, reserved for pedestrian traffic. The Civil Forum was separated from the market by a large four-sided arch faced in marble and stucco and adorned with statues. On the north side of the commercial part of the forum a singular complex has been unearthed, preceded by a portico of columns and pillars, with a whole row of shops. Above there were at least two other floors with rental lodgings.

House of the Mosaic of Neptune and Amphitrite

This house belonged to an unidentified wealthy cultured merchant, who exercised his trade in the large shop that opened onto the street and was in communication with the rest of the building. Furnished with great care, the shop has come down to us in an excellent state, with the wares still on the counter and wine amphorae neatly lined up on a shelf. Entrance to the tablinum is from the atrium, followed by a summer triclinium with a triclinial masonry table faced in marble and with the walls covered with fine mosaics. A nymphaeum with a central apse niche is on the back wall. There are smaller rectangular alcoves on either side, and the facade is covered by a glass paste mosaic. Four vines wind up to the architrave of the side alcoves from four vases (*cantaroi*) set at the base of the alcove jambs. Two elegantly framed hunting scenes with garlands of leaves and fruit above begin at the architrave. The wall at the side of the nymphaeum has the mosaic picture after which the house is named and shows *Neptune and Amphitrite* framed in an imaginative and elaborate architectural composition. The rooms on the upper floor still have part of their pictorial decoration and furnishings.

▼ *View of the Decumanus Maximus at the crossing with Cardo V*

▲ *The summer triclinium of the House of Neptune and Amphitrite with the lovely mosaic after which the house was named*

▶ *The atrium of the Samnite House*

Samnite House

This is one of the oldest houses in Herculaneum and in part still looks as it originally did in the latter decades of the 2nd century BC. A carefully made sidewalk runs along in front of the facade. The elegant portal with jambs in tufa blocks and Corinthian capitals leads into the fauces, with decoration in *First Style* (polychrome stucco rustication imitating marble). The atrium is of particular interest, with an elegant loggia of Ionic columns in the upper part. A charming stuccoed marble screen fills in the spaces between the columns. The rooms on the ground floor with their fine decoration give us an idea of the original patrician characteristics of the house. The upper floor was later transformed into small rental apartments, with an independent entrance in the form of a small wooden staircase.

◀ *The imposing Tuscan atrium of the House of the Wooden Partition*

tablinum gives onto a small garden with a portico with small pillars, on which some of the rooms and the triclinium open.

House of the Mosaic Atrium

The entrance and the atrium are paved with mosaics. The *tablinum*, on an axis with the other two rooms, is closed at the back and divided into three aisles by two rows of pillars. The other rooms are at the side and are oriented towards the sea to make the most of the view. A portico with windows, with the garden at the center, joins the atrium to the triclinium and the other official rooms. On the eastern side of the portico are four cubicles with red-ground paintings, placed on either side of an exedra finely decorated with architectural paintings and with scenes of the *Punishment of Dirce* and *Diana at the bath*, both in airy landscapes.

House of the Wooden Partition

Dating to the Samnite period, it was considerably changed in Augustan times. The well-preserved facade is of particular interest. Around the middle of the first century the house, originally an elegant and noble patrician residence, was partitioned into rental lodgings for families who shared various common services. A second floor was built over the atrium while some of the rooms overlooking the street were turned into shops. The large Tuscan atrium with the impluvium, where rainwater was collected, is particularly majestic. From here access could be gained to the cubicle to the right of the fauces, with a floor mosaic in geometric pattern. A marble table found on the upper floor, set on a statuette of the Phrygian divinity *Atthis* as a base, is now here. The house takes its name from the large wooden partition that separated the atrium from the tablinum, two thirds of which is still extant (one of the two doors with three wings is missing). This must have been a fairly common element in Roman houses, but since wood is not durable, the fact that it survived here is quite unusual. The cases in the atrium and in the tablinum contain objects found in the house, including dried legumes. The

▶ *The atrium of the House of the Mosaic Atrium with the floor, after which the house was named, paved in black and white squares*

▶ *The portico of the north side of the Palaestra*

At the end of the house, beyond the triclinium, is a loggia and a terrace. Two small pavilions that served as belvedere flank the loggia. Many wooden parts of the house were found and have been put in their proper place, including a cradle and a small wooden table.

Palaestra

The entire eastern part of Insula II was taken up by a large palaestra, with a large open space at the center in which were a cruciform swimming pool of considerable size and another smaller one. A portico with columns ran along three sides of this open area while there was a cryptoporticus on the fourth. The palaestra, with two monumental entrances, one on Cardo V and the other on the Decumanus Maximus, had a whole series of accessory premises for various uses.

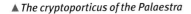

▲ *The cryptoporticus of the Palaestra*

▶ *The bronze fountain with the five-headed Serpent wrapped around a tree trunk, in the large cruciform pool of the Palaestra*

House of the Relief of Telephos

This is one of the most aristocratic dwellings in the southern part of the city, despite the irregularities in the layout, due above all to the nature of the land on which the building stands. An airy vestibule leads into the atrium that is divided into three aisles by two rows of columns, with marble *oscilla* decorated with theater masks and figures of satyrs hanging between them. The tablinum is at the back of the atrium. On the left two small doors lead to the rustic part, which also has stables (*stabulum*) with a very low ceiling. The remaining part of the house, with a different orientation, is on a lower level and is reached by going down a sloping corridor next to the tablinum. A large peristyle with brick columns surrounds the spacious garden. Another corridor leads to a panoramic terrace on which other rooms open. One of these is of astonishing beauty in the luxurious decoration in precious marble. The neo-Attic relief with the *myth of Telephos* (or of Orestes) after which the house is named was found in a small room near this hall.

House of the Deer

Dating to the Claudian-Neronian period, the house is rationally divided into two distinct zones, the entrance, with atrium and triclinium, and the other one with panoramic terraces, reached by means of a large portico with windows. The entrance (*fauces*) leads into a modest atrium that lacks both the opening in the roof (*compluvium*) and the tub for collecting rainwater (*impluvium*). Next comes a large triclinium with the walls soberly

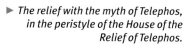

▶ *The relief with the myth of Telephos, in the peristyle of the House of the Relief of Telephos.*

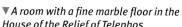

▼ *A room with a fine marble floor in the House of the Relief of Telephos*

decorated by fine architectural structures and other motifs on black ground and with a pavement in tiles of different types of marble. The two famous marble sculptures of *Deer at bay*, found in the garden of the house, are on view here. There are two small rooms in the same part of the building, at the center of one is a marble statuette of a *satyr with a wineskin*. The vast quadriporticus has no columns but consists of four arms of a covered corridor with windows, en-

▲ *The southern facade of the House of the Deer*

◄ *Statue of a satyr with a wineskin, in the House of the Deer*

▼ *Deer attacked by dogs, one of the two sculptural groups after which the house was named*

closing the garden, a large triclinium and two day rooms. The quadriporticus was decorated with pictures of varying subjects, many of which were detached and are now in the Archaeological Museum in Naples.

▶ *The base of the honorary monument
to M. Nonius Balbus,
proconsul of Crete and Cyrene*

Suburban Quarter

The suburban area stretched out towards the sea beyond the city walls and with its aristocratic residences and public buildings supplied the old city with greater breathing space. In the southwestern part a few powerful vaulted substructures probably supported terracing. The sacred area, rectangular in shape, was comprised of closed rooms and an open space where the religious rites for a congregation were held. More terracing follows, including the terrace of Marcus Nonius Balbus (his funerary ara was found here), which led to the Suburban Baths.

On the northwestern part, beyond the present Via Mare, various buildings and complexes have recently been brought to light. They were already known in the eighteenth century, but can now in part be seen for the first time, considerably extending the area of the Archaeological Park of Herculaneum.

◀ *The caldarium of the Suburban Baths*

Suburban Baths

The baths are at the far southern edge of the city. The entrance consists of a portal with columns supporting a triangular pediment. A few steps lead to a vestibule with a shaft skylight supported by four columns with smooth shafts on which round-headed arches rest. The fine marble herm of *Apollo* is still here. It is supported by a pillar from which water ran into a basin in front. From here there is access to the various parts of the baths, all well preserved. There were no separate sections for men and women and it may have been used only by men, or by both sexes on alternate days. A single room, most of which is occupied by the swimming pool, served both as *apodyterium* and *frigidarium*. Between the *tepidarium* and the *frigidarium* there is a room elegantly decorated with stuccoes and marble and with marble seats along the walls, probably a sort of waiting room. The *caldarium*, as usual, has a tub for hot water of modest size and a basin for cold water ablutions. The room for the furnaces that heated the baths, the *praefurnium*, is behind the *caldarium*. In recent decades the skeletons of some of the

fugitives who had sought shelter in the vaulted structures that faced the beach have been found.

Northwestern Insulae

The *insulae*, located beyond the Via Mare, are composed of groups of buildings that are hard to place. One large room with an apse however seems to have been a swimming pool (*natatio*) with nymphaeum, probably part of a bath complex that has not yet been studied. Covered by a gabled roof, the large room has a series of structures inside that served to heat the water, while above a facing in tiles with projecting studs (*tegulae mammatae*) is visible. These created a cavity in the wall up which hot air could rise, keeping the temperature of the room constant.

A house with a large vaulted room has also been identified. The room had *Fourth Style* paintings, and a relief in Greek marble with a *Young Satyr, nymph and satyr*, of neo-Attic style, at the center of the south wall. This is a rare example of a specific type of mixed decoration in which marble reliefs are surrounded by painted surfaces and we know from Cicero that it was greatly appreciated by particularly cultured and refined intellectuals in the first century BC (the only other example known is in Pompeii, in the House of the Golden Cupids).

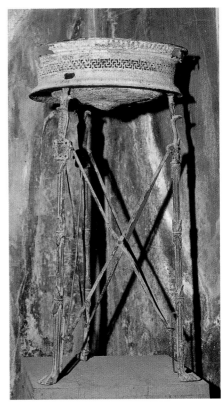

▲ *Bronze brazier in the Antiquarium*

Antiquarium

The statue of the Egyptian god *Athum* and the marble statue of the *child Eros* are the most noteworthy of the numerous everyday objects and various fine works of art unearthed during the excavation. A new complex is planned in which to exhibit the wooden relic of the Roman boat found in 1982 on the ancient beach of the city, upside down and well preserved up to the rudder. The two main parts of the museum are to be as unobtrusive as possible.

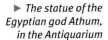

▶ *The statue of the Egyptian god Athum, in the Antiquarium*

Villa of the Papyri

Still further north, with respect to the Archaeological Park of Herculaneum, parts of the famous Villa of the Papyri have now been opened to the public. Discovered by chance in 1750 it was then studied by means of tunnels and shafts by Karl Weber and his successors. All the shafts had to be closed in 1765 on account of gas fumes and it was not until 1980 that new excavation campaigns were begun. During that first campaign 87 sculptures dating to the first century BC were recovered (copies of Greek originals of the 4th and 3rd century BC, now in the Archaeological Museum in Naples) and 1000 papyrus scrolls, most of which contained Greek texts on the Epicurean philosophy of Philodemus of Gadara. The philospher, present in 1st century BC Rome and connected to the circle of Lucius Calpurnius Piso Caesoninus, Julius Caesar's father-in-law and consul in 58 BC, may have been the owner of this extensive complex, that seems to have been all of 250 meters long.

The purpose of the new excavation campaign undertaken in 1980 was to unearth what Weber had discovered and accurately surveyed in his plan of the so-called *Belvedere*, the circular structure at the end of one of the villa paths (from which comes a famous floor now in the Museum in Naples), and in the plan of the entire area, with indications of where the objects found were located. Modern studies have demonstrated the accuracy of Weber's plan, which was subsequently used by Paul Getty, the American millionaire, in the construction of his villa in Malibu-

Los Angeles, now headquarters of the Paul Getty Foundation. Since 1991, thanks to a first series of open excavations (no longer underground) allowing the public to participate in the discoveries, the areas excavated by Weber are being reopened

and connected to the archaeological area of Herculaneum. The complex of the Villa of the Papyri, datable to 60-50 BC, was laid out on at least three levels, in a panoramic site overlooking the sea. On the lowest level, in the southwestern area, the so-called *basis villae* has now been brought to light. This large earthwork, plastered white outside and with numerous rooms in-

side, was the base for the terraced structures above (there are remains of painted decorations with vines and pictures with animals and cupids in the inner rooms). Above, a second terracing had a curved forepart, probably for the view towards the sea. The "New Excavations", carried out between 1996 and 1998, have uncovered only the area of the atrium (also surveyed by Weber), since the rest of the complex is in lands that have not yet been expropriated, beneath the modern city of Resina. Despite the fact that the atrium, the main entrance to the villa, was in the principle terraced area and therefore higher than the other two, geological changes made the dig extremely difficult. Since the coastline was sinking, the aquifer had risen and the entire site was subject to flooding so that pumps were required to drain off the water. Sixteen rooms have been uncovered in the atrium quarter behind an entrance composed of a portico with columns on three sides, oriented towards the coast, as in the Villa of Mysteries in Pompeii (therefore a common plan in Campania). The portico leads to the atrium itself, with at the center the impluvium basin surrounded by fountains. From here, once the dig continues, one should reach – at least according to Weber's eigh-teenth-century plans – a first peristyle with various rooms at the sides (including the library where the famous papyrus scrolls were found). The enormous garden peristyle, almost 100 meters long and with a large swimming pool at the center, should be located to the west of the first peristyle, passing through the large exedra of the tablinum in the form of an *ephebeum* (hall furnished with seats) to a gymnasium. In the eighteenth century many of the statues now in Naples were found under the porticoes and in the open. Lastly the Villa presumably ends in the long path with the Belvedere at the top, previously identified by Weber. At present the visit is limited to the quarter of the atrium, where the entrance ambulatory has an interesting mosaic decoration with regular black tessera pattern on the floor. The facing of the principal triclinium, with white tessera mosaic, a central carpet with polychrome windmill blades, and on the walls, the remains of *Second Style* painting are visible in the rooms open to the public.

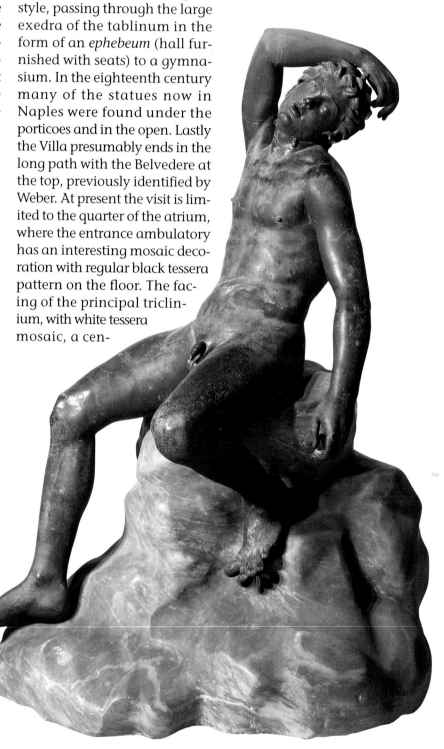

▶ *Sleeping satyr, now in the Archaeological Museum in Naples. This lovely bronze statue, a Roman copy of a 3rd century BC Greek original, was found in the second half of the eighteenth century in the peristyle of the suburban Villa of the Papyri*

OPLONTIS
Torre Annunziata

The excavations of Oplontis, also buried in the eruption of AD 79, are at the center of the modern city of Torre Annunziata, making it difficult, as in the case of Herculaneum, to proceed with archaeological research. Actually it was not a city by itself, but rather a sort of hamlet of Pompeii (it may even have been a suburban area). It was in other words a wealthy "suburb", characterized by noble villas. In the Tabula Peutingeriana, a sort of geographical map of the roads in Italy during the late Roman Empire, copied in the Middle Ages, we find the place name "Oplontis" although it is not clear if it indicates a thermal building or a villa. Moreover in the first century BC the historian Strabo mentioned that the entire Campanian coast "from Miseno to Sorrento looked like a single city". Located 3 miles both from Pompeii and from Stabiae, and 6 from Herculaneum, Oplontis for us today corresponds principally with the remains of the so-called "Villa of Poppaea" (or Villa A), so well-known that it was named a World Heritage Site by UNESCO. The rustic villa attributed to Lucius Crassus Tertius (or Villa B) and a bath structure are also in the center of Oplontis.

Villa of Poppaea (or Villa A)

It was during the excavation of a canal in the 1700s that the remains of this important settlement were intercepted. Up to 1840 a series of tunnels were dug but poisonous fumes and the lack of funds brought the ex-

▶ *Portico of the north peristyle*

▼ *The colonnade of the northern viridarium*

▲ *The corridor that connected the core of the villa with the part with the pool*

cavation to a halt. The Bourbon state bought the area anyway, in view of future excavations. A century was however to pass be-fore they were once again begun systematically and scientifically in 1964.

The ownership of this large villa, extremely rich and articulated, has been attributed to Poppaea Sabina, second wife of the em-peror Nero, because of an in-scription painted on an amphora, addressed to "Secundus", a freed-man of Poppaea. Even if it did not belong to the empress, the villa, dating to the first century BC and uninhabited at the time of the eruption of AD 79 since it was being restored, must still have been part of the imperial properties. All that remains of the oldest part of the complex, set higher than later buildings, is a wing overlooking a large gar-den, consisting of a projecting body flanked by porticoes. The main entrance of the house has not been excavated because it

◀ *Detail of the corridor ceiling decorated with a geometric pattern*

▲ *Detail of pictorial decoration in the Second Style*

is under the modern center. Between the 1st century BC and the first century AD a series of annexes went up around that core. They include a bathing quarter, spacious gardens and a *palmentum*, where grapes were pressed. The inner residential rooms, in view of the suburban site of this complex, are decorated with rich paintings in the *Second Style*, with false doors and columns, perspective plays but also masks, baskets of fruit, birds (themes common also to the *Third Style*) all characterized by a marked "illusionistic realism". After an earthquake and shortly before the fateful eruption, many rooms were about to be newly decorated with the "fantasy" that marked the *Fourth Style*. The villa also had numerous sculptures, Roman copies of Greek Hellenistic masterpieces, now no longer *in situ*.

▶ *Detail of the fresco in the reception hall, on the western side of the Villa of Poppaea*

◄ *Detail of pictorial decoration in Second Style in a room next to the large atrium*

Villa of Lucius Crassus (or Villa B)

In 1974 during the construction of a school a few hundred meters from the Villa of Poppaea the remains of a second large suburban residence, arranged around a peristyle in two levels, came to light. It was a rustic villa attributed to "Lucius Crassus" (as an inscription tells us) and in which, in addition to numerous bodies of victims of the eruption, a real treasure was found in 1984, the so-called "gold of Oplontis". This hoard, now in Naples, consists of 170 gold and silver coins and various particularly fine examples of the goldsmith's craft (jewelry, bracelets, rings and earrings), typical of the area and the Roman world in the early part of the Empire. Much of the villa has not been excavated because of the modern houses above, but we know that, in addition to the area of the peristyle, it consisted of an extensive series of other annexes.

▼ *The elegant wall decoration of the triclinium*

VESUVIUS

With its characteristic cone, Mount Vesuvius is one of the principal landmarks in the landscape around the Gulf of Naples. This active volcano, 1277 m. high, rises up from the old volcanic enclosure of **Mount Somma** (1132 m.). Historically Vesuvius first appeared on the scene in AD 79 when, a few years after an earthquake, it erupted and buried the neighboring cities under a sea of ashes and lapilli: Pompeii, Herculaneum, Stabiae. The Latin historian Pliny the El-der, who entered the disaster zone out of scientific curiosity, was both spectator and victim. His nephew, Pliny the Younger, at the time eighteen years old, re-ported the tragic events of the

▼ The great cone of Vesuvius

people who lived around Vesuvius. Eruptions have continued since then, the last in 1944. The area around Vesuvius has been famous since antiquity for its fertile lava soil, for its vineyards, which produce an excellent *Lachryma Christi*, and for the lovely 18th century villas in the towns around the volcano. An excursion to the crater is of great interest both for a sight of the spectacular cavity and for the marvelous panorama of Naples and the coast.

◀▼ *Three impressive shots of Vesuvius: the volcano during the last eruption of 1944; the river of lava; the crater*

NAPLES

With its mild climate, art and architecture, beautiful setting, excellent cuisine and picturesque nooks and crannies, Naples is unquestionably one of the loveliest of Italian cities. It was founded by the Greeks around the 7th century B.C. as Parthenope (after a mythical siren), and the name was later changed to Neapolis (New Town). In Roman times it was famed as a vacation site, although it remained a highly cultured Greek city in appearance and customs, with more than its share of theaters. Nero and Lucullus were among the famous men who lived there, as well as Vir-gil who is also buried there. In the 6th century it fell under Byzantine rule where it remained (formally at least for it was actually fully autonomous) until 1139, when it became part of the Norman kingdom. In the Middle Ages it ranked as the most important of the Campanian cities and the history of the region and that of Naples were in a sense one and the same. The Swabian Hohenstauffen dynasty (13th century) succeeded the Normans and with Frederick II the city became an important center of art and culture. Between the late 13th and 14th century under the House of Anjou its standing increased. It was then that the Maschio and Castel Sant'Elmo were built and outstanding artists such as

▲ The "Guglia dell'Immacolata", spire in Piazza del Gesù Nuovo

▼ Panorama of the famous Via Caracciolo and Castel dell'Ovo and with Vesuvius in the background

▼ *Piazza del Municipio in front of the Maritime Station of Naples*

▲ *View by night of the Basilica of San Francesco di Paola in Piazza del Plebiscito*

Simone Martini, Pietro Cavallini and Tino di Camaino, as well as famous writers such as Boccaccio, were drawn to Naples. In the 15th century power passed to the House of Aragon and in the 16th century the Spanish troops arrived and the Kingdom of Naples was ruled by Spanish viceroys. Culturally and economically the period of prosperity lasted till the early 17th century. The aborted popular revolt led by Masaniello dates to 1647. In 1656 the plague killed over 400,000 Neapolitans. The Bourbons became the new arbiters in the 18th century and cultural and artistic activity blossomed with the construction of the Capodimonte Palace and the adjacent porcelain factory whose products soon became famous throughout Europe, with the music of Cimaro-

▼ *The long straight street known as "Spaccanapoli"*

▲ *The "Carciofo" (artichoke) Fountain in Piazza Trieste e Trento*

▼ *Shepherds in a typical Neapolitan crêche*

sa and Pergolesi, and the philosophical thought of Giovan Battista Vico. Then in the 19th century the brief period of Napoleonic rule was followed by the reign of Murat and the restoration of the Bourbons. In 1860 Garibaldi arrived and Naples was annexed to the Kingdom of Italy. Recent history includes philosophers like Croce, the theater, both in dialect and in Italian, from Scarpetta to the De Filippo family, and the four heroic days during which Naples was liberated from the enemy occupation of 1943.

▲ *A typical lane in Naples*

▲ View of the Gulf of Naples

◀ Palazzo Donn'Anna in Posillipo

The Gulf of Naples

It is hard to know where to look in this lovely gulf with its unique views, where sky and sea merge on the horizon and with Mergellina, Posillipo, Marechiaro, the island of Nisida. The visitor leaving Naples is haunted by a sense of wistfulness and promises in his heart to return.

▲ The island of Nisida

◄ *The nineteenth-century facade of the Cathedral of San Gennaro*

► *The exhibition of the Relic of Saint Gennaro when the blood liquefies*

Cathedral

Built in the 13th century and subsequently transformed, the facade, except for the three Gothic portals (1407) decorated with reliefs by Antonio Baboccio, dates to the 19th century. Inside, entrance to the **Chapel of San Gennaro** or **Treasury**, is in the right aisle. This Baroque masterpiece dates to the early 1600s and was frescoed by Domenichino and Lanfranco. It contains the famous relics of the blood of Saint Gennaro (Januarius), patron saint of the city. In May and September crowds gather to witness

► *The interior of the Cathedral*

▲ *Chapel of San Gennaro or Treasury*

▶ *The precious reliquary-bust of Saint Gennaro*

the miraculous liquefaction of the blood contained in the two phials. A chapel in the transept contains an *Assumption* by Perugino. The **Cappella Minutolo** and the underground **Cappella Carafa** with the 16th century *statue of Cardinal Carafa in prayer* are also of interest. In the left hand aisle is what remains of the **early Christian Basilica of Santa Restituta**, and the **Baptistery** with 5th century mosaics.

San Lorenzo Maggiore

Built by the Franciscans between the 13th and 14th century, this is one of the loveliest of Neapolitan Gothic churches. It was here that Boccaccio met Fiammetta (his muse) in 1334. Petrarch lived here in 1345, in the annexed convent.

The interior has a nave only, with side chapels. Among the works of art are a 14th century wooden *Crucifix*, the *tomb of Catherine of Austria* by Tino di Camaino (c. 1325), the *tomb of Robert of Artois and Joan of Durazzo* (1399). The cloister (18th century) and the remains of Greek and Roman buildings can be reached from the church.

▲ *The facade of San Lorenzo Maggiore*

◄ Bird's eye view of the Maschio Angioino

▼ View of the Maschio Angioino and detail of the Arch of Triumph of Alfonso I of Aragon

Maschio Angioino

Known also as **Castel Nuovo**, the dungeon was built by the Angevins around 1280. Re-stored in the early 1900s, it now looks as it did after the Aragonese modifications of the 15th century. It was the seat first of the Court of Anjou, then of the Arago-

▶ *The Arch of Triumph between the Torre di Mezzo and the Torre di Guardia*

nese court and finally of the Spanish viceroy. The entrance to this massive castle with its large cylindrical towers consists of the majestic **Triumphal Arch** built for Alfonso I (1443) and decorated by sculptors from varying places. Of interest inside is the **Palatine Chapel** or **of Santa Barbara** and the **Hall of Barons**. Fourteenth-century frescoes as well as works by Mattia Preti, Solimena, Vincenzo Gemito and Caracciolo are in the *Museo Civico* of Castel Nuovo. Guglielmo Monaco's finely sculpted *bronze door* of around 1475 is also in this museum. A cannon ball is embedded in the lower left panel.

▼ *The bronze door by Guglielmo Monaco*

▶ *Detail of the second attic of the Arch of Triumph with the four Virtues and two river gods*

Galleria Umberto I

This impressive and elegant gallery, with its daring glass and wrought-iron roof and its typical belle époque aspect, dates to the end of the 19th century. At the time galleries of this type were being built in various other Italian cities. Famous personages such as D'Annunzio, Salvatore di Giacomo, Scarfoglio, etc. used to meet here in the **Teatro Margherita**.

◄ *Galleria Umberto I*

Palazzo Reale

▼ *View of Piazza Plebiscito with the Basilica of San Francesco di Paola, flanked by the hemicycle portico and the Royal Palace*

Begun in 1602 by Domenico Fontana for the viceroy's court, Joachim Murat later also stayed in the palace. The broad porticoed facade overlooks **Piazza Plebiscito**. The **Grand Staircase** leads to the **State Apartments**, with elegantly decorated

◄ The Royal Palace from the back

▼ A fine room in the Royal Palace

rooms, furniture, 17th and 18th century paintings of Neapolitan school, furnishings and tapestries. Of interest is the **Court Theater** (1768) by Ferdinando Fuga. The building is also the seat of the **National Library** and contains, among others, a collection of papyri from Herculaneum.

▲ The Grand Staircase leading to the State Apartments

▲ *The Throne Room in the Royal Palace*

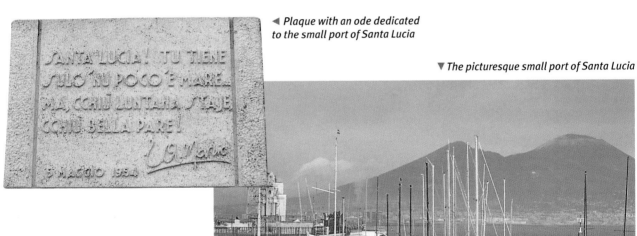

◀ *Plaque with an ode dedicated to the small port of Santa Lucia*

▼ *The picturesque small port of Santa Lucia*

Castel dell'Ovo

The castle stands on the picturesque rocky islet of **Borgo Marinaro**, with its old fishermen's houses and famous restaurants overlooking the small **port of Santa Lucia**. It was built in the 12th century over a Basilian monastery that stood on the site of the Roman villa of Lucullus. The name derives from a me-

▲ *Borgo Marinaro with the massive Castel dell'Ovo*

dieval legend according to which Virgil (thought at the time to have been a magician) had hid- den a magic egg (*ovo*) here, with catastrophic results were it to be broken. The massive walls en- close towers, dungeons, Gothic halls and a few cells from the old convent.

▲ *Remains of the Roman villa of Lucius Licinius Locullus, the initial core of Castel dell'Ovo*

◄ *The massive structure of Castel dell'Ovo, now also used for exhibitions and meetings*

Castel Sant'Elmo

This is one of the keys for a historical understanding of Parthenope, for from its imposing bastions an eye could be kept on what was happening in the city below and any enemies who might appear on the horizon. The strategic site appealed to the Angevins who built the fort in the first half of the 14ᵗʰ century. The present star-shaped plan dates to modifications carried out for the Aragonese by the Viceroy Pedro of Toledo. For some time, the castle, initially known as **Belforte**, was a military prison but has now been given over to civil use. It contains the **Church of S. Elmo** (16ᵗʰ cent.) and the 17ᵗʰ century **Chapel of S. Maria del Pilar**. The castle drill grounds offer one of the finest panoramas around.

▲ *General view of Castel Sant'Elmo and the Certosa of San Martino*

Certosa di San Martino

The monastery dominates the city from the Vomero hill, in a splendid panoramic position. It was built in the 14ᵗʰ century by Tino di Camaino and other architects, commissioned by the House of Anjou, and then remodeled in the 17ᵗʰ century by Cosimo Fanzago in Baroque style. It is now the premises of the **Museo Nazionale di San Martino**. The 16ᵗʰ century church, by Dosio and Fanzago, is splendidly decorated with marbles, sculptures and 17ᵗʰ century paintings of Neapolitan school. These include a *Deposition* by Massimo Stanzione, Ribera's *Prophets*, *The Washing of the Feet* by Battistello

◄ The vaulting of the Sacristy

Caracciolo, works by Vaccaro, Reni and Solimena. There is a fresco by Luca Giordano in the **Treasury Chapel**. The Museum also contains the collection of 18th century **Nativity Scenes** or **Christmas Cribs**, one of the most interesting and characteristic expressions of Neapolitan art; the **Picture Gallery** with works by Solimena, Salvator Rosa, Caracciolo, Luca Giordano and 19th century Neapolitan artists; the **Sculpture Section**, with works by Tino di Camaino, Sammartino and Pietro Bernini; the **Minor Arts Section**, with Murano glass and Capodimonte porcelains. The **Great Cloister** of the convent (16th-17th century) is magnificent.

▼ The Baroque interior of the Church

▲▼ *The lovely Large Cloister*

San Domenico Maggiore

Built in the 13th and 14th centuries, San Domenico is a good example of Angevin Gothic architecture, despite various renovations. The church apse gives onto the square of the same name, with, at the center, the Baroque votive monument known as **Guglia di San Dome-** nico or St. Dominic's spire, built in 1658 to mark the end of an epidemic of the plague. Inside, in the **Cappellone del Crocifisso**, with a frescoed vault, is a 13th century *Crucifix*, said to have spoken to Saint Thomas of Aquinas. There is a fresco by Solimena (1709) in the sacristy as well as works by Luca Giordano and the school of Tino di Camaino.

▲ *The Baroque votive monument or* "Guglia di San Domenico"

▶ *The interior of San Domenico Maggiore*

► *Disillusion, by Francesco Queirolo*

Cappella Sansevero

Built between 1590 and the middle of the 18th century by the Sangro family, the chapel is decorated with magnificent sculptures: *Disillusion* by Francesco Queirolo, *Modesty* by Antonio Corradini and the *Veiled Christ* by Giuseppe Sammartino. A room nearby contains two macabre but interesting examples of experiments in the mummification of cadavers carried out by one of the princes of Sangro.

▼ *Modesty, by Antonio Corradini*

► *Veiled Christ, by Giuseppe Sammartino*

▲ *The premises of the National Archaeological Museum*

▼ *Ephebus, from Pompeii*

Archaeological Museum
(Museo Archeologico Nazionale)

With its rich documentation of Greco-Roman art and countless finds from Pompeii, Herculaneum and Stabiae this is one of the largest and most important archaeological museums in the world. Founded in the 18th century by the Bourbons, the premises are in a large 16th century palazzo, formerly a barracks and subsequently University premises. On the museum ground floor are the ***Marble Sculptures:*** among those of note, the famous group of *Tyrannicides*, Roman copy of the Greek orig-

▼ *The Battle of Darius and Alexander, Pompeian mosaic*

▶ *Aphrodite Sosandra, from Stabiae*

▼ *Fresco depicting Spring, from Pompeii*

▼ *Portrait of Paquius Proculus and his wife, from Pompeii*

▼ *Pompeian mosaic with itinerant musicians*

inal by Kritios and Nesiotes (5th cent. B.C.); the relief with *Hermes, Orpheus and Eurydice* (5th cent. B.C.); the statue of *Athena,* copy of an original of the school of Phidias; the *Doryphoros* from Pompeii, one of the finest copies of the original by Polycleitus; the *Ephebus,* also from Pompeii, copy of a 5th century B.C. original; the *Callipygian Venus,* after a Hellenistic original; the *Farnese Bull,* from Rome, copy of a Hellenistic original; the *Aphrodite Sosandra,* from Stabiae. The **Mosaics,** all from Pompeii, are in the mezzanine: the great *Battle of Darius and Alexander; marine fauna,* with a fight between an octopus and a lobster; *Roving Musicians; Plato's Academy; Scene of Magic.* On the upper floor are the finds from the *Villa of the Papyri* in Herculaneum, with statues and paintings. The **Collection of Paintings** includes: the portraits of *Paquius Proculus and his wife,* from Pompeii; many still lifes; *Diana Huntress* and the so-called *Spring,* delicate paintings from Stabiae; *Knucklebone Players,* a monochrome from Herculaneum; *Theseus and the Minotaur,* from Pompeii; *Hercules and Telephos,* from Herculaneum. Of interest also the **Collection of Precious Objects,** the **Secret Cabinet** (special permission required) which contains erotic subjects, and the **Technology Section,** with tools and devices.

▼ *Hercules and Telephos, from Herculaneum*

Palazzo Reale di Capodimonte

The monumentality, size and imposing architectural conception of this building, with pilasters vertically articulating the facade surmounted by a balustrade, justify its name as **Palace of Capodimonte**. Charles III of Bourbon commissioned it from Giovanni Antonio Medrano and Antonio Canevari (1738). This sovereign also founded the famous **royal porcelain manufactory**, active in the first half of the 18th century. It was subsequently dismantled and set up

▲ Palazzo Reale di Capodimonte

elsewhere, and eventually closed in the early 19th century. All around is the splendid Park (the former **Woodlands of Capodimonte**), with breathtaking views of the city framed by the gulf. The initial installation of the first nucleus of works that now make up the **Museum** and the **National Galleries of Capodimonte** was begun by Charles of Bourbon, who had first of all to see to the Farnese collections. Subsequent donations, the acquisition of important private collections, as well as the need to find a safe place for works in some of the city's churches, made this mu-

▲ Porcelain coffee service in the Museum of Capodimonte

◀ *Annunciation, by Titian*

▲ *Sala della Culla*

seum one of the most important in southern Italy, in particular for the internationally famous picture gallery. It contains works by Tuscan, Umbrian, Venetian, Emilian, Lombard, foreign and – obviously – Neapolitan artists of varying periods and importance. A special section is devoted to 13th to 19th century Neapolitan artists, together with painters of other schools active in Naples. Among the most important, mention must be made of the *Crucifixion* (Masaccio), *Robert of Anjou Crowned by St.* *Louis of Toulouse* (Simone Martini), *Portrait of Francesco Gonzaga* (Mantegna), Portrait *of Paul III Farnese* (Titian), *Virgin and Child with angels* (Botticelli), *Madonna of the Assumption* (Masolino da Panicale), *Transfiguration* (Giovanni Bellini), *Flagellation* (Caravaggio), *Mystical Marriage of St. Catherine* (Correggio), *Sacra Conversazione* (Palma the Elder), *Madonna of Humility* (Roberto d'Oderisio), *Resurrection* (Sodoma), *Atalanta and Hippomenes* (Guido Reni), *The Blind Leading the Blind* (Pieter

▲ *Danae, by Titian*

▼ *Salone delle Feste*

▲ *Flagellation, by Caravaggio*

Brueghel), *Youth Lighting a Candle with a Coal* (El Greco), *Crucifix* (Antonis van Dyck). There are also precious objects, small bronzes, gold work, ivories and silverwork, including the *Farnese Coffer*. Particularly noteworthy in the **Royal Apartments**, with porcelains, various furnishings and fine furniture, is the *Porcelain Parlor* (second half 18th cent.). Decorative arts, works in porcelain and majolicas are the fulcrum of the **De Ciccio Collection**. In the **Tapestry Gallery** are fine pieces from the 16th century Belgian manufactory. One section is reserved for contemporary masters, with Alberto Burri, Mario Merz and Andy Warhol in the forefront.

◄ *The Porcelain Parlor of Queen Maria Amalia of Saxony*

► *Saint Gennaro and Saint Peter, fresco in the Catacombs of San Gennaro*

Catacombs of San Gennaro

Entrance to the catacombs is by the **Madre del Buon Consiglio Church**. One of the largest complexes in southern Italy, these catacombs are outstanding for the number of wall paintings, dating up to the 10th century. They date back to the 2nd century and are arranged on two subterranean levels. Of note among the frescoes is the one depicting *St. Gennaro*, of the 5th century, when the remains of the patron saint of the city were put there.

◀ Detail of the fresco with Saint Gennaro, in the catacombs of San Gennaro

first skeletons date to after the plague of the 16th century) were placed in some of the tufa quarries and, in line with a curious folk custom, were cleaned and venerated by the families of the district. The **Catacombs of San Severo** with 5th century frescos are near the church of S. Severo.

Catacombs of San Gaudioso

Entrance is from the Crypt of the **Church of S. Maria della Sanità**. This cemetery dates to the 5th century and contains the *Tomb of St. Gaudioso*. The mosaics and frescoes range from the 5th to the 6th centuries. In the 17th century portions of the catacombs were used in a rather unique way, for the cadavers were set to dry on hollow seats. When they were later walled up, the skulls were left visible, while the wall was decorated with subjects that commemorated the deceased. The **Ossuary of the Fontanelle** is also located in the Sanità district. A considerable number of bones and skulls (the

▶ Gallery in the Greek area of the Catacombs of San Gennaro

▲ *Entrance to Naples Underground*

ters. The effects of this millenary activity however have also been deleterious. Indeed, every so often a chasm opens up unexpectedly in the city streets. For an exciting experience, all one has to do is make advance reservations for a guided tour: "Napoli Sotterranea", Piazza San Gaetano, 68.

▼ *Fascinating pictures of Naples Underground*

The City Underground

One of the entrances to the fascinating world of underground Naples is in the **Church of San Paolo Maggiore** where a portion of what is believed to have been the **Augustan Aqueduct** can be visited. Water was brought from Sarno to the wells in the city. The conduits were around 170 km long. The tour goes through a series of tunnels and cisterns of uncertain date and unspecified use. The custom of digging into the subsoil in the area, including the excavation of building material, goes back to prehistory. The Greeks and Romans in turn kept up this custom, which continued throughout the centuries. In World War II the underground cavities served as air raid shel-

SORRENTO

Famous seaside resort on the gulf of Naples, Sorrento stands on a tufa bank rising sheer from the sea. It was already a favorite vacation site with the Romans. In the Middle Ages it was Byzantine, then an independent duchy and Norman. Attacks by Saracen pirates were frequent. The poet Torquato Tasso was born here in 1544. The area abounds in citrus plantations, while silk and lace are some of the typical craft products. The **Cathedral** (considerably rebuilt in modern times) stands at the

▼ A picture of the enchanting Sorrentine coast

◄ The Sedile Dominova, an interesting fifteenth-century loggia in Via San Cesareo

▼ Frescoes in the dome of the Sedile Dominova

crossing of **Corso Italia** and **Via Tasso**, the main city streets. Of note inside are a *bishop's throne*, a 16th century *pulpit* and a 15th century *Adoration of the Child*. The **Basilica of Sant'Antonino** is also of interest. It is medieval but was renovated in Baroque style. The *Tomb of the Saint* can be seen in the crypt, where an oratory existed as far back as the 14th century, later incorporated into the basilica. The interior, with a nave and two aisles, has numerous 17th century paintings and a fine **Nativity scene** or crèche in the sacristy, an example of 18th century folk art by the greatest Neapolitan sculptors of this genre. A visit to the *Sedile Dominova*, an elegant 15th century loggia, is also to be recommended, as well as to the **Church of San Francesco** and its charming *cloister* with Moorish interlaced arches dating to the 14th century. But above all go and see the **Museo Correale di Terranova**, installed in the 18th century palazzo of the counts of Terranova. The museum contains an extraordinary collection of minor arts (majolicas, Baroque Neapolitan furniture, Capodimonte porcelains and clocks) and paintings of Campanian school. Near Sorrento, at **Punta del Capo**, are the remains of the Roman **Villa of Pollius Felix**, rising up sheer over a tiny picturesque "cove" with tall rock cliffs on either side of the narrow passageway.

◄ Remains of the Villa of Pollius Felix

POSITANO

For those arriving from Sorrento, the most enchanting and picturesque stretch of the Costiera Amalfitana or Amalfi Coast begins at Positano. The winding panoramic road snakes its way along between the Mediterranean macchia and the steep cliff walls that loom overhead, offering exquisitely beautiful views at every curve. After still another curve, there is Positano, almost a dreamlike vision, a rare flower protected, set into the harsh slope of the mountain, in correspondence to a tiny but sheltered ocean bay. Originally a fishing village, it developed after the inhabitants of Paestum took shelter there to escape the Saracen raids. In the years of the "Dolce Vita" it became a gilded hideaway for the jet set. Today the picturesque lanes are lined with elegant shops, boutiques carrying designer brands, fashionable locales, exclusive meeting places and luxury hotels. The enchanting houses, cascading down in superposed rectangles and cubes with charming loggias and the inevitable terraces above – almost an icon of the Mediterranean landscape, seem to come straight from a fairy tale. After leaving the car in one of the car parks along the road that moves off from the

▼ The picturesque hamlet on the bluff with the sea below

▲ *Panorama of Positano
from the Spiaggia Grande or Large Beach*

Costiera, a brief walk takes the visitor to the *Spiaggia Grande* or Large Beach with its annexed small harbor. One of the loveliest views of Positano and the coast is to be had from here, framed by the **Torre Trasita** (one of the numerous lookouts along the Costiera). The sea-front is dominated by the **Parish Church** **of Santa Maria Assunta,** in Baroque style and crowned by a delightful majolica dome. Inside is a Byzantine thirteenth-century panel painting of the *Virgin and Child* and a *Circumcision* by Fabrizio Santafede.

AMALFI

The Amalfi Coast is one of the most famous tourist areas in Italy. It includes the Sorrentine Peninsula from Sorrento to Salerno, and is one steep ravine after another, with stretches of coast falling sheer down to a deep blue sea, and with beaches and characteristic towns overlooking marvelous inlets. Amalfi is a stupendous tourist town, one of the most popular in Italy thanks to its beauty and art. Founded by the Romans, it reached its maximum splendor in the Middle Ages. As a free Republic (the oldest of the Italian Maritime

◄ *View of Amalfi*

▼ *An enchanting view of the town and the bell tower of the Cathedral in the foreground*

Republics), it long dominated commerce in the Mediterranean with its fleet, contributing to the history of navigation with the first maritime code, the *Tavole Amalfitane*, and perfecting the compass (by Flavio Gioia). Defeated and sacked by Pisa, it began to decline in the 12th century. Every year a crew takes part in the historic **Regatta of the Maritime Republics**. The principal monument in the city is the **Cathedral**, founded prior to the 9th century and remodeled more than once. It stands in a scenic position at the top of a tall flight of steps. The two-colored facade with its varied forms is a 19th century renovation in Gothic style. The upper part of the bell tower (12th-13th century) is in Moorish style, with majolica revetment. An extraordinary *bronze*

▲ *The splendid facade of the Cathedral*

▼ *The Tavole Amalfitane, in the Municipal Museum*

▼ *The interior of the Cathedral*

◄ *The portico with its pointed interlacing arches around the Chiostro del Paradiso*

door on the main entrance was made in Constantinople around the middle of the 11th century. Inside the church are two *Romanesque pulpits*, an ancient *baptismal font* and, in the crypt, the remains of the apostle Saint Andrew. From the Cathedral access is to the delightful **Chiostro del Paradiso**, built in 1268 in Moorish style with pointed interlacing arches. Interesting archaeological finds are on exhibit under the portico.

▼ *Amalfi seen from the port*

▼ *The viewpoint of Villa Cimbrone with a splendid panorama of the Costiera*

RAVELLO

▼ *Villa Cimbrone with its magnificent gardens*

Almost tucked away from the traffic along the Costiera, Ravello stretches out on a slope between the Dragone and the Regina valleys. In the thirteenth century the site, with a prosperous trade with the East and Sicily, was at its zenith to which the architecture of many buildings, with their unmistakable Arab-Norman features, still bear witness. The icon of Ravello, reached via a fork shortly after Atrani, is the famous view of the small **Church of the Annunziata** (13th cent.), from the gardens of Villa Rufolo. The two small bell towers, with their cupolas in Arab style, frame a breathtaking backdrop, with Mediter-

▶ *The thirteenth-century Gospel ambo, by Niccolò di Bartolomeo (Cathedral of Ravello)*

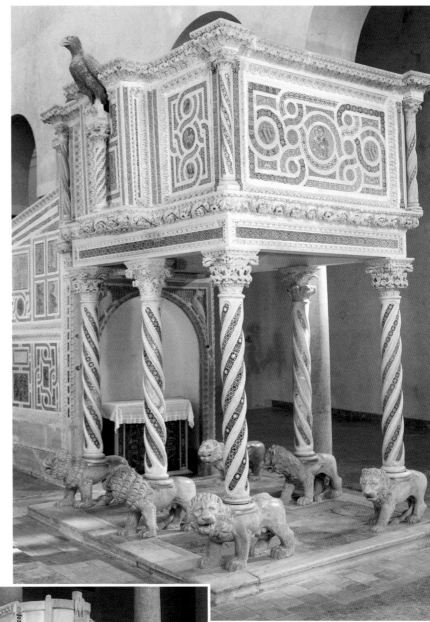

ranean pines, luxuriant vegetation, fabulous coast and cobalt blue sea. A square **Tower**, at the edge of *Piazza Vescovado*, leads to the **Villa Rufolo** (13th-14th cent.), a complex of buildings bound to the memory of Richard Wagner (who lived there and to whom a summer festival is dedicated) and characterized by Norman-Islamic architecture, of particular note in the large windows of the cloister and the tower of the main building. The *gardens*, set on various levels, offer botanical rarities and a fantastic panorama. Another gem of Ravello is the **Villa Cimbrone**, built by an Englishman who was enthusiastic about the Grand Tour. It has a magnificent *Park*, with one of the most enchanting viewpoints of Southern Italy. The **Cathedral of San Pantaleone** (11th century with Baroque renovation) has a bronze *portal* by Barisano da Trani (12th cent.), a fine *ambo* in Byzantine style (on the left side of the nave) and

the thirteenth-century *Gospel ambo* (on the right) by Niccolò di Bartolomeo (13th cent.). The **Cathedral Museum** is in the crypt. Among other outstanding highlights of Ravello are the **Church of San Giovanni del Toro** (12th-18th cent.), the **Camo Coral Museum** and the old churches of **Santa Chiara** and **San Francesco**, restructured in the eighteenth century.

◀ *Byzantine ambo with two flights of steps with mosaic decoration (Cathedral of Ravello)*

▲ *An enchanting view of the Costiera from the gardens of Villa Rufolo in Ravello*

CETARA

A characteristic seaside hamlet, Cetara overlooks the Costiera Amalfitana, at the mouth of the Vallone Grande, in sight of Punta Fuenti. The name would seem to derive from the Latin *Cetaria* (tuna net) or from "*cetari*", the sellers of large-size fish. In the ninth century the coastal settlement was an outpost for the Saracens who were besieging Salerno. Subsequently conquered by Amalfi, it passed under its rule, but in the second half of the sixteenth century it was taken by the Turks who massacred the civilian population. Modern Cetara retains the typical buildings of coastal fishing hamlets. The cubical houses, with barrel vaulting or cupolas, cluster around the old lookout **Tower**. The **Church of San Pietro** is of note for its fine majolica dome and is flanked by a thirteenth-century bell tower with an octagonal belfry.

VIETRI SUL MARE

▼ *Flowers and fruit vendors, two details of the typical Vietri ceramic ware*

The last town on the Costiera before Salerno, Vietri stretches out along its gulf, at the foot of Monte San Liberatore and at the mouth of the Torrente Bonea. The origins of the place seem to go back to *Marcina*, an Etruscan site mentioned by Strabo, and apparently in trade relations with *Nuceria*. Burials with tomb furnishings in archaic Corinthian ceramics have been found here and in the area, as well as the remains of Roman baths (Marina di Vietri), and a wall in *opus reticulatum*, now under water, near Punta Fuenti. The local economy has been based on the artisan working of ceramics ever since the Middle Ages. A **Ceramic Museum**, with finds and documentation from the eighteenth to the twentieth century, has been installed in *Villa Guariglia* in località Raito. The seventeenth-century **Mother Church of San Giovanni Battista**, with a fine majolica dome, and a sixteenth-century *Polyptych* is in the main town. A sixteenth-century defensive **Tower** is near the Marina.

PAESTUM

Paestum is one of the most important archaeological sites in Italy. It was founded by Greek colonists in the 7th century BC and was named *Poseidonia*, or city of Poseidon. By the time the Lucanians conquered the town at the end of the 5th century BC and changed the name to *Paistom*, it had already achieved a prominent position throughout the plain of the Sele river. In 273 BC it became a Roman colony, one of the most flourishing and faithful in the Latin world. Its fortunes waned in the early Middle Ages, when the harbor was silted over and malaria became rife. In the 9th century Saracen raids convinced the last few inhabitants to abandon the site. Paestum was overrun by vegetation and forgotten until the 18th century and the most recent excavations. It now offers visitors a vast archaeological area with streets, the remains of dwellings, theaters, baths and splendid Doric temples. Archaeological finds are on exhibit in the Museum. The **Temple of Ceres**, actually dedicated to Athena, was built at the end of the 6th century BC. There are thirteen columns on the long sides and six on the front and back where the pediments and architraves are also still in existence. The cell inside is preceded by a *pronaos* of which the column bases are still extant. In the Middle Ages the temple was transformed into a Christian church. The **Temple of Neptune**,

◀ *The Temple of Ceres*

▼ *The Temple of Neptune*

▲ *The Basilica*

built around the middle of the 5th century BC and dedicated to the Argive Hera, is among the most beautiful and best examples of Doric architecture. It is of imposing size and elegance: the columns, with their accentuated entasis or curve, have a warm golden hue, spellbinding at sunset. The **Basilica** is the oldest temple, dating to the middle of the 6th century BC and was dedicated to Hera. It still has its entire portico of fifty columns.

▼ *The Amphitheater*

CAPRI

apri is one of the most famous Italian tourist resorts in the world, crowded in all seasons. The island rises up as a mass in a deep blue sea, with its splendid Mediterranean vegetation and deeply indented coastline, riddled with grottoes including the famous **Grotta Azzurra** or Blue Grotto, one of the loveliest in Italy. A small opening on the sea leads into a large space with an extraordinary blue light, where objects plunged into the water take on silvery tones. **Capri** is the island's main center, a charming picturesque town

◀ *The fascinating interior of the Grotta Azzurra or Blue Grotto*

▼ *The famous town square of Capri*

with low houses, winding streets, hotels and shops. It is particularly animated at New Year's with its famous popular festival. Other centers are **Marina Grande**, **Anacapri** and **Marina Piccola**. A small resort and bathing center on the southern coast, Marina Piccola is the point of departure for excursions by boat to the **Faraglioni**, enormous rocks rising up out of the clear sea.

▲ *The imposing Faraglioni*

◄ *The natural arch rising sheer on the east coast of the island*

▼ *View of Marina Grande*

ISCHIA

The wealth of mineral springs, fumaroles and spas on Ischia can be traced back to the volcanic origins of the island. The beauty of the landscape and the coast, together with the mild climate and the spas, attract a great number of tourists in all seasons. The fertile soil has favored the growth of splendid pine groves, citrus plantations and grapes. The Greeks who first colonized it in the 7th century BC called it *Pithecusa*. Then came the Neapolitans and Romans who made the most of it as a vacation resort. Subsequently it belonged to the Normans, the Angevin and the

▲ *The picturesque fishermen's hamlet*

▶ *Panorama of Ischia from the Aragonese Fortress*

Aragonese and was frequently devastated and sacked by the Saracen pirates (which is why so many lookout towers were built). Ischia is the most important center on the island, divided into two parts. **Ischia Porto** stretches out with its elegant streets, hotels and spas around the port, which is set in a volcanic crater. **Ischia Ponte** stands in the area of the **Aragonese Bridge**, built in 1438 to join the picturesque fisherman hamlet to the islet on which the **Aragonese Fortress** and the former **Convent of the Poor Claires** stands.

▼ *The Aragonese Fortress*